it's easy
here's how

Kerstin Martensson

1st Printing . . . . January, 1969

2nd Printing . . . . June, 1969

3rd Printing (Revised) . . . . October, 1969

4th Printing . . . . February, 1970

5th Printing . . . . April, 1970

6th Printing . . . . July, 1970

7th Printing . . . . September, 1970

8th Printing . . . . February, 1971

9th Printing . . . . April, 1971

Printed in the United States of America

Kerstin Martensson is one of the best-known home economists in the western world and undoubtedly one of the best-traveled. Since 1965 she has made five trips to the United States and Canada and has lectured in a total of 43 states to home economists in schools, colleges and universities. She has demonstrated the latest sewing technics at the last three National Home Economists Conventions which were held in San Francisco, Dallas and Minneapolis. Prior to her first visit to the United States she worked in England, Germany, Norway and Denmark.

Kerstin was born and educated in Gothenburg, Sweden, where she specialized in clothing construction, pattern designing and fashion. She attended *Göteborgs stads Verkstadskola* and *Stockholms Tillskärar Akadimi,* and as a part of her education was required to spend three years in practical training in the sewing and designing industries of Sweden. During this period she conducted evening classes in clothing construction for the Gothenburg School System.

She was employed by the exclusive *Wettergren Salon* in Gothenburg in 1958 in the capacity of Supervisor where she designed original fashions for customers and supervised their construction.

In 1960 she became associated with Husqvarna Vapenfabriks of Sweden, one of the largest sewing machine manufacturers in the world. This gave her an opportunity to fulfill a lifetime dream of traveling around the world as well as a chance to observe sewing technics used in these various countries. She conducted training classes at the factory for home economists from Sweden, England, Iceland, Greenland, Denmark, Norway, Finland, Germany and other countries to bring them up to date in the latest technics of sewing the newest fabrics, and to acquaint them with developments of the most up-to-date sewing machines. In addition, she

designed garments which were shown in fashion shows she promoted throughout Sweden.

Kerstin's distinguished career also includes television and radio appearances throughout the United States and other countries. In addition she has made films on sewing, one of which is called "Sewing Stretch Fabric" which is currently being used in many schools throughout the United States and Canada. This was the first film ever made which dealt exclusively with the technics of sewing stretch fabric at home.

Kerstin is currently the Program Director for the Sew-Knit-N-Stretch Corporation. In addition to her other duties she has designed exclusive patterns for them specifically for knit and stretch materials.

The home sewing industry is deeply indebted to Kerstin for her efforts in writing this long-awaited book. We know it will open up a whole new world to women who will now be able to successfully sew garments in the new knit and stretch fabric.

Robert F. McMaster
President
Sew-Knit-N-Stretch, Inc.

This book could not have been written without
the inspiration and assistance of Carol Guzy,
whose creative writing ability changed my poor
English into an understandable language.
Carol attended the University of Minnesota and is
employed as an executive secretary. She has a
flair for expressing herself in writing that is
precise and easily understood.
This is essential for a book of this kind.

Kerstin Martensson

Illustrations by Judith Meyeraan

Judith Meyeraan attended the University of Minnesota
and the Minneapolis School of Art. She is a free-lance
fashion artist and has done work for leading fashion
stores throughout the midwest area.

It's easy to see why home sewing has changed
during the past few years. Sewing has had to
change with the times, like everything else, in
order to keep up with our continuing fast pace
of life. Necessity is the mother of invention and
these new knit and stretch fabrics are no
exception. They reflect the need for garments
that can be made easily and quickly, yet they
must fit properly and be comfortable; for garments
that are easy to care for, yet durable; for
garments that are attractive, yet within the price
range of everyone.

This was a rather tall order to fill, but the answer
came with the advent of knit and stretch fabrics
and the resulting development of proper sewing
technics. This combination — marvelous new
fabric and simple sewing technics — has rekindled
the interest in sewing that has been missing
for so many years.

Table of Contents

As in any new method, there are certain principles that can be generally followed for working with knit and stretch fabric and in this chapter we will attempt to outline them.

These principles are easy to learn and will soon dispel the idea that sewing with knit and stretch fabric is difficult or "tricky". On the contrary, we think you'll agree that sewing with this type of fabric is easier and faster than sewing with any other type of material. In fact, sewing and fitting need be no more of a problem than cutting out the pattern.

With today's large families and the increasing rise in clothing costs, now the housewife and mother is able to sew garments for her entire family — skillfully and economically — and at the same time get a lot of satisfaction and enjoyment out of the professional-looking garments she is able to make. Creative talent, of course, can be beautifully expressed as you will see when you use your imagination in adding individual touches to the clothes you sew.

Just remember these simple, basic rules when you sew with knit and stretch fabric and you will be well on your way to modern sewing at home. And when you have made a beautiful sweater in less than thirty minutes, you'll be glad you started sewing with this fantastic fabric.

Knit and Stretch Fabric

Knit and stretch fabric meets every requirement for active, modern people. It's ideal for action-wear garments where the fabric must be able to give with body movements. It's made to order for people who travel extensively.

You do not have to line garments made from knit and stretch materials. Lining them would, in fact, defeat the purpose as it would limit the stretch factor, thus restricting freedom of movement.

Generally speaking, the greater stretch of the fabric should run around the body, or horizontally. Ski pants, however, are one exception because here the stretch should go up and down, or vertically, in order to get freedom for leg movements such as bending, jumping, etc.

Knit and Stretch fabrics are made from wool, cotton and various synthetic fibers. There are many methods used in the knitting process. Two of the most popular methods are "double knit" and "single knit." You can tell the difference because a double knit fabric looks almost the same on both sides while a single knit fabric looks smoother on the right side, the wrong side has a more uneven texture.

As far as caring for garments made from knit and stretch material, we suggest dry cleaning for wool; machine washing is satisfactory for cotton (if the fabric has been pre-shrunk), and usually synthetic materials can be laundered by hand or machine. Before cutting and sewing cotton knit, it is advisable to preshrink it yourself — wash it in hot water — since cotton knit that is not pre-treated will shrink.

Synthetic fibers are divided by generic (or family) names. Manufacturers, in turn, designate the fabric they make from this particular fiber by another name. The following chart will give you an idea of some of the many brands that are made from four well-known synthetic fibers. This may help clarify the technical-sounding terminology sometimes used to describe synthetics.

Popular synthetic fibers used in knit and stretch fabrics

Generic Name	Familiar Brands	Characteristics
Acrylic (Polyakryl)	Acrilan, Orlon, Courtelle, Dralon, Creslan	Soft, wool-like fiber, warm, requires minimum care
Nylon (Polyamide)	du Pont Nylon Enka Nylon, Perlon (Germany), Grilon (Switzerland), Amilan (Japan), Nyfil (Mexico), Rilsan (Italy)	Strength, elasticity, quick-drying, easy care
Polyester	Dacron, Kodel, Fortrel, Terylene (England), Trevira	Good resiliency, wrinkle-resistant, quick-drying, requires minimum care
Spandex	Lycra, Vyrene	Excellent elasticity, lightweight, quick-drying

If you are in doubt as to fiber content of fabric,
you may take a single strand of the yarn and
burn it. The following chart indicates how certain
fibers burn or melt and what the resulting
ash looks like.

Reaction of various fibers to flame

Fiber	Reaction to Flame
Acrylic	Burns and melts. Leaves hard, crisp, black ash.
Nylon	Melts very slowly with small flame. Leaves round, grey, hard ash.
Polyester	Slowly burns and melts. Leaves hard, black, round ash.
Spandex	Melts. Leaves black, fluffy ash.
Wool	Burns slowly (smells like burnt hair). Leaves black, soft ash.

Patterns

In order to sew knit and stretch fabric successfully, you must use a suitable pattern. There are patterns on the market today that are designed especially for knit and stretch fabric. There is a big difference that distinguishes these patterns from regular patterns, the difference being that patterns for knit and stretch fabric are designed specifically for fabric that *stretches*.

Naturally not all knit and stretch fabric has the same degree of stretchability. Generally, fabrics can be classified as having a low, medium or high stretch factor. You must take this into consideration when you select your pattern and you should know for what type of fabric the pattern was designed.

The patterns referred to throughout this book are SEW-KNIT-N-STRETCH patterns made exclusively for knit and stretch fabric. These

patterns are designed for fabric with a medium stretch factor. Therefore, if your fabric is very stretchy, make the garment smaller; if the fabric has a low stretch factor, use a larger size pattern. SEW-KNIT-N-STRETCH patterns have three to four sizes in each pattern envelope and each pattern has a simplified, step-by-step instruction sheet, complete with illustrations. The pattern pieces are printed on heavy-duty paper thus making them easier to handle and much more durable.

There is an arrow on each Sew-Knit-N-Stretch pattern piece indicating the proper grain of fabric which is important in obtaining the proper stretch to your garment. Measurements are given in centimeters as well as inches on these patterns.

Cutting

As you arrange your pattern pieces on the
fabric, bear in mind that you are now working
with resilient material. Therefore, use a large table
and make sure the fabric does not hang over
the edges. This would cause the fabric to stretch
and your fabric pieces may not be exact.

Hold the pattern pieces to fabric with pins or
heavy weights. We recommend the weights since
they can be handled faster and will not pull the
fabric as pins sometimes do. Anything will do to
use as weights — look in your kitchen cupboards
(cans, knives, heavy coasters) — as long as it is
heavy enough to hold the pattern piece to fabric.

When cutting knit and stretch fabric, always
use a sharp pair of scissors. Dull scissors will
shred the fabric edges making it difficult to
sew the ¼″ (6 mm.) seam allowances sometimes
called for.

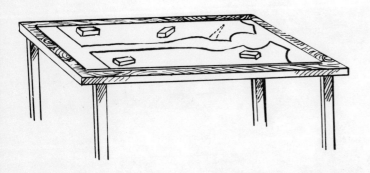

Fitting

Getting the proper fit used to be one of the biggest problems in sewing. Knit and stretch fabric has all but eliminated this problem because it virtually fits itself.

It's a proven fact that no one's body is exactly the same on both sides. If you had separate pictures of the right and left sides of your body you might be surprised at the differences you would observe. Some differences are very slight — some more noticeable — and some can indeed present a fitting problem. For example, it's very common to have one shoulder lower or one hip higher. Knit and stretch fabric automatically adjusts to most of these differences with no effort on your part at all.

You may have to make some adjustment in a pair of slacks or a skirt. This is easily accomplished by putting the garment on and tieing a string around your waist (over the garment). Now stand in front of a mirror. If you are fitting a skirt, pull the fabric up slightly under the string, adjusting it so it hangs properly. For slacks, pull the fabric up under the string until the crotch fits properly, even when you bend over. Mark the string position with pins or chalk and you have your exact waistline.

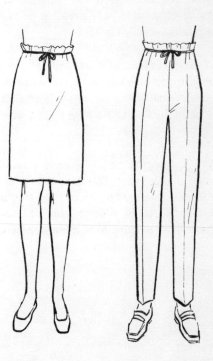

Sewing

Many people do not realize that you can sew knit and stretch fabric with any kind of sewing machine. Naturally, some machines work better for this particular type of fabric than others. However, we suggest you use the following methods for whichever type of machine you will be using.

For all sewing machines you should loosen the pressure on the presser foot when sewing knit and stretch fabric, except when sewing swimsuit and ski pants fabric. Then use normal pressure.

For all sewing machines your thread tension should be balanced. This means that the upper and lower thread tensions are equal and the stitch looks the same on both sides of the fabric. When you have the thread tensions in balance, the stitch knot is in the middle of the fabric and is relatively invisible.

Balanced Stitch

We suggest you get in the habit of holding the bobbin and top threads taut behind the sewing machine needle as you begin to sew. This will prevent the soft fabric from pulling down into the needle plate.

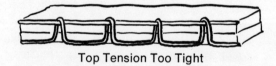

Top Tension Too Tight

One of the most helpful aids to you will be the roller presser foot. This foot rolls smoothly over the fabric without catching the loops in sweater material. We recommend using the roller pressure foot when sewing all knit and stretch fabric.

Top Tension Too Loose

The sewing machine we have found that sews knit and stretch fabric most efficiently is the Viking sewing machine (called HUSQVARNA in many countries). This sewing machine has seams designed especially for knit and stretch fabric in addition to a wide variety of other seams. It has a "Colormatic" system for selecting the seams you desire simply by turning three dials to the same color. For example, the BLUE-BLUE-BLUE setting (a serging-type seam), overcasts and sews the pieces together in one operation. This seam is very similar to seams on ready-made garments. It's ideal for sewing knit and stretch fabric where you often have a narrow seam allowance and, as the stitch is elastic, it stretches with the fabric so you never have to worry about the seam breaking.

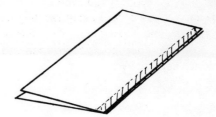

The Viking (Husqvarna) sewing machine also has an elastic straightstitch (YELLOW-YELLOW-ZERO) and an elastic blindstitch (ORANGE-ORANGE-ORANGE) which eliminates hemming by hand. The elastic straightstitch has triple-lock strength and is ideal for sewing seams where extra stress can be expected — perfect for action-wear garments. The elastic straightstitch is also recommended for sewing darts.

If you are using ⅝" (1½ cm.) seam allowance, overcast the edges separately with the three-step zigzag stitch which has three stitches in each zig and zag.

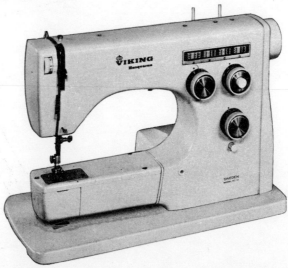

If you have a zigzag machine, you can still sew knit and stretch fabric satisfactorily by using a zigzag stitch. You will get a fairly elastic seam by setting the stitch length and stitch width at medium (not too large). When using ¼" (6 mm.) seam allowance, we suggest you overcast the seam allowance together to prevent raveling, and use a large zigzag stitch to avoid rippling. For ⅝" (1½ cm.) seam allowance, press seam open and overcast edges separately.

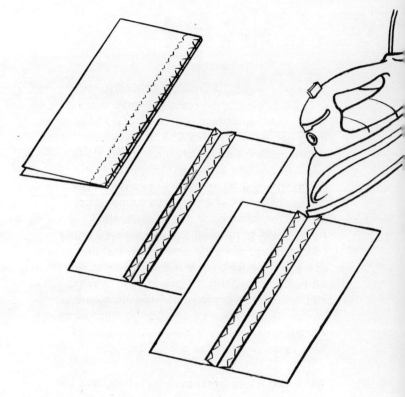

It's impossible to get an elastic seam on a straight stitch machine, but you can still sew knit and stretch fabric by sewing the seam two or three times, stretching the fabric as you sew. Your stitch length should be slightly longer than normal. Overcast the seam allowance by hand to prevent raveling.

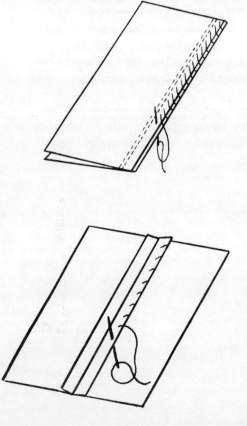

Pressing

To press knit and stretch fabric, you should use
a steam iron. Do not press hard — just touch
iron lightly on the fabric and let the steam
do the work for you.

Get in the habit of pressing each seam as
you sew it. No matter how wide your seam
allowance is, first press flat with right
sides together to eliminate rippling.

Then, if using ¼″ (6 mm.) seam allowance,
press seam toward one side.

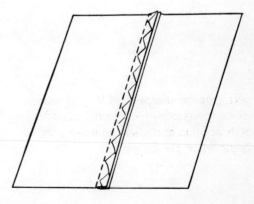

If using ⅝″ (1½ cm.) seam allowance,
press the seam open.

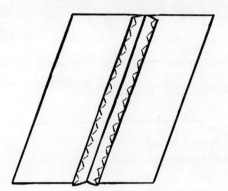

To prevent press marks from showing on the
right side of garment, press under edge of seam
allowances after you have pressed the seam.

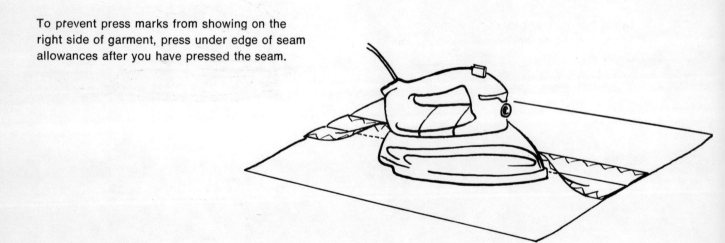

To make creases sharper and longer-lasting
(in slacks, for example), dampen a cloth
in starch solution and place between iron
and fabric when pressing.

Hemming

Never use seam binding for hems in knit and stretch fabric. Seam binding will not stretch and therefore could cause the hem to pucker.

Overcast edge of fabric if necessary. Sew hem with elastic blindstitch on your sewing machine.

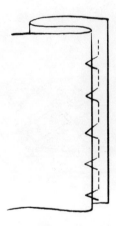
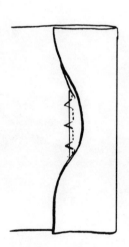
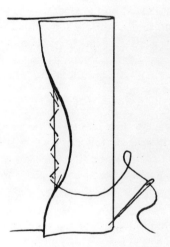

If you sew the hem by hand, do not stitch on the very edge of fabric, but under the edge about ¼" (6 mm.). Be sure to keep your thread loose. If you sew the hem too tightly, the hem will pucker or the thread will break.

Finish your hem by steam pressing and be sure to press under the ¼" (6 mm.) edge to eliminate press marks showing on right side of garment. This will make your hem invisible from the right side.

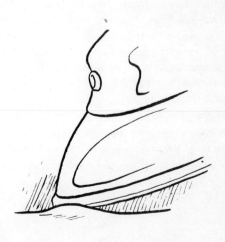

Recommended Sewing Aids

Pins

We have found a special pin that will not become tangled in the sweater fabric — that holds securely until you remove it — and that is very easy to handle. This pin is shaped somewhat like a hairpin (see diagram).

We do not recommend sewing over any pins. There is always the possibility of your sewing machine needle hitting a pin, breaking off and causing some injury.

Weights

The quickest and easiest way to hold pattern pieces to the fabric when cutting is to use heavy weights, especially when cutting sweater fabric which is sometimes bulky.

Pressing Ham

A pressing ham can be of tremendous help for knit and stretch fabric especially where you have to form-press (the neckline of a sweater, for example). If you use it just once you'll see the big difference it makes.

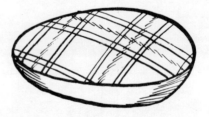

"Scotch" Magic Transparent Tape

This tape has so many uses (as you'll see in reading this book) that we recommend keeping a roll close at hand whenever you are sewing. One of the many advantages of using this particular brand of tape is that you can write on it (it has a dull finish, not glossy). For example, when you have several small pieces cut out, you can put a piece of "Scotch" Magic Transparent Tape on each piece and mark what piece it is. You can also sew through this tape when making buttonholes without having to worry about your needle getting sticky.

Thread

For sewing knit and stretch fabric, you may use mercerized cotton thread or a good synthetic thread. We have tested various brands of thread and found one we feel is superior in every way. This thread is fairly new to the American market and is called SPUN SYNTET, manufactured by Molnlycke, one of the leading thread manufacturers in Europe.

SPUN SYNTET can be successfully used for sewing every type fabric and compared with mercerized cotton thread, it is
— 25% stronger
— 50% more elastic
— ten times more durable in friction tests.

In addition, SPUN SYNTET retains its high ratings at extreme temperatures which makes it excellent for sewing swimsuits and ski pants. This thread never shrinks, does not change color under artificial lights, is strong enough for buttons, yet fine enough for sewing lingerie.

SPUN SYNTET is highly recommended for its unsurpassed all-around performance and high quality.

Whatever thread you use, be sure your bobbin and top thread are of the same quality.

Roller Presser Foot

This presser foot is ideal for sewing with knit and stretch fabric. It is available with either a high or low shank and can be used on almost every sewing machine on the market today.

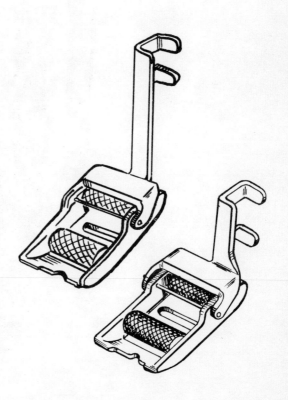

Personal Notes — Sewing Technics

Sweater fabric comes in a large variety of
shapes, sizes, textures and fibers. Some sweater
fabric is knitted in the shape of a tube (called
a sweater body); some is knitted flat (called
sweater blanket); some is in the form of yardage.

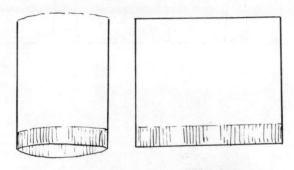

There is usually a "run" in the sweater body
depending on the knitting method used. This is
not a flaw in the sweater body itself, but is
a result of the knitting process. Cut the sweater
body open on this "run" to avoid any defects
in your sweater.

Sweater bodies and sweater blankets have
one edge finished with ribbing. Sweater yardage
does not, although it is very suitable for making
dresses, suits and coats. It can also be used for
sweaters, but you have to finish the bottom
of sweater and cuffs by hemming or by
using special trim.

Some sweater bodies and sweater blankets are
large enough to make a complete sweater,
or you may have to use two smaller ones in order
to make one sweater. Be sure to keep this in mind
when you are purchasing your sweater fabric.

If you are using two sweater bodies (both the same size) to make one sweater, the best way to get the sweater out of these two bodies is to take the back and one sleeve on one sweater body and the front and one sleeve on the other sweater body. However, some manufacturers produce sweater bodies in two sizes — one for the back and front; one for the sleeves.

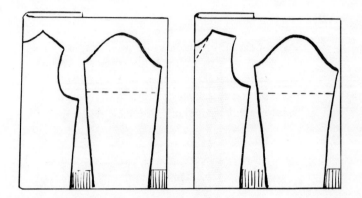

Designed Sweater Bodies

Some sweater fabric is partially designed; some has an all-over design. This type of fabric makes a beautiful sweater, but you have to cut the pattern pieces more carefully.

When cutting a sweater with a partial design, cut out the sleeves first. Measure the distance from the design to under-arm point. Line up the back and front pattern pieces so the distance from design to under-arm point is exactly the same, then cut back and front pieces.

This same procedure is used for a sweater with an all-over design. Have the design exactly the same at under-arm point on sleeves and back and front pieces.

The most popular type of sleeves in sweaters are raglan sleeves and set-in sleeves.

Keep in mind that a sweater with raglan sleeves requires a longer sweater body or blanket than a sweater with set-in sleeves.

If you are making an extra large man's sweater and the width of the sweater material is not sufficient, you may cut the sleeves a little narrower by tapering top of seam on both sides or by folding the pattern piece in the middle, lengthwise.

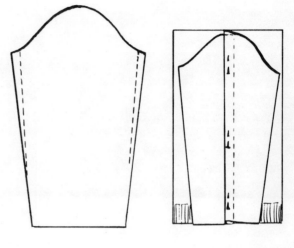

Before you cut the fabric, check your measurements with the pattern to get correct length of body and sleeves and proper stretch of fabric. If you decide to use a separate cuff, remember to cut the sleeve shorter depending on the length of the separate cuff.

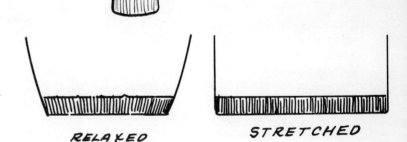

To get a ribbed finish at bottom of sweater and cuffs, place the bottom of these pattern pieces on the ribbing. Stretch the ribbing before you cut it or it may be easier for you to remove the pattern piece when you have cut to about 1" (2½ cm.) of ribbing. Then finish cutting using the grain of fabric as a guide.

RELAXED   *STRETCHED*

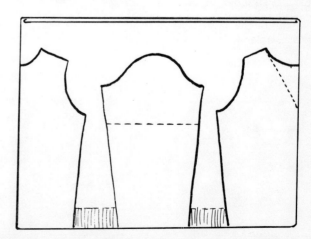

If you find your fabric is too short,
you can place the shoulder of the
pattern pieces as near top edge of fabric
as possible so that the bottom will have a
finished edge. Your sweater will now be
shorter than the pattern.

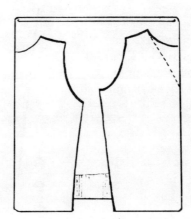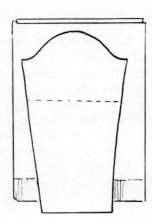

If you are making a short sleeve pullover
using a SEW-KNIT-N-STRETCH pattern, just
place dotted line on pattern piece on the
ribbed edge. For three-quarter length sleeves
(or other lengths), measure length you
desire, mark your pattern piece accordingly,
and place this on the ribbed edge.

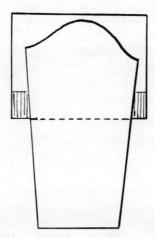

On a raglan sleeve pullover, the back shoulder seam is longer than the front shoulder seam. To avoid sewing the sleeves in backwards you should indicate which is the back and front shoulder seam. The easiest way to do this is to place a piece of "Scotch" Magic Transparent Tape about 1″ (2½ cm.) from edge of shoulder seam and mark on tape "Back" or "Front."

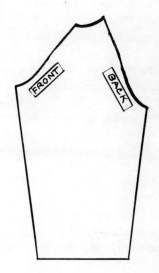

If you are making a sweater of loosely-knitted fabric, you may end up with sleeves that are too long because of the greater stretch factor in this loosely-woven fabric. To avoid this, after you have cut out the sleeves, shake them and then place the pattern piece on ribbed finish. You may find that as a result of this shaking, you have to trim excess fabric at top of sleeves.

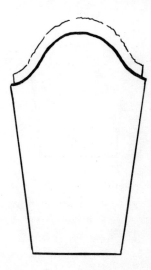

Sew the shoulder seams of your sweater first.

To keep the shoulder seams on a sweater with
set-in sleeves from stretching, you can attach
non-stretch seam binding to the shoulder seams,
particularly when your sweater fabric is loosely
knitted or when making a man's sweater.
You may also unravel four or five threads from
the fabric itself. Stretch the threads and
steam press to remove krinkles. Then when you
sew the shoulder seams, place these threads
under your presser foot and sew them into the
seams. This actually looks more professional
and you will not have to buy extra seam binding.

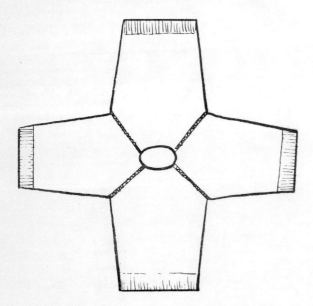

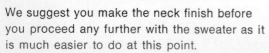

We suggest you make the neck finish before
you proceed any further with the sweater as it
is much easier to do at this point.

Round Neck

(The same method is used for making a
MOCK-TURTLENECK or a TURTLENECK.)

Cut the neckband as wide as you desire,
depending on the style you choose. You can use
the following suggested widths as a guide:

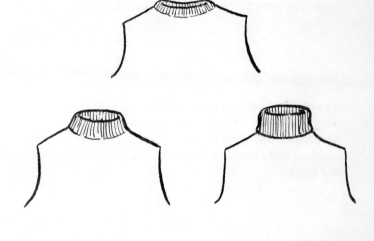

      Round Neck . . . . 2½″ (6 cm.)
      Mock Turtleneck . . . . 4½″ (11 cm.)
      Turtleneck . . . . 9½″ (24 cm.)

Cut a straight piece of sweater fabric or
ribbing, as wide as desired (decide if you want
neckband single thickness, double or folded)
across the grain. A strip 18″ (46 cm.) long is
usually sufficient.

You may use a ribbed neck finish, knitted in
a circle, which also can be used for any width
neckband you desire. If you use a ready-made
collar which is not circular, join the ends together
to form a circle by placing the ends together and
sewing a zigzag seam so your needle alternately
catches each end.

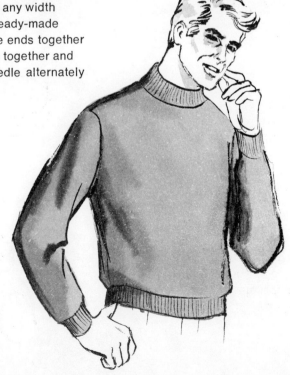

To get correct size for your neckband, stretch the band very tightly around head, then move the band to neck and check for comfortable fit. Cut off excess, making sure to allow for seam allowance.

Sew band together to form a circle. If you are making a folded turtleneck, sew half of the seam on the wrong side, half on the right side. Now when you fold the turtleneck, no raw edges will show.

If your ribbing has no finished edge, fold and press band lengthwise, wrong sides together.

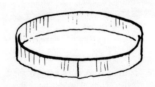

Divide neckband and neck opening in fourths with pins.

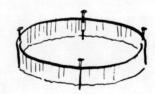

Pin band to neck opening on right side, raw edges together, by matching pins. Stretch neckband to fit neck opening as you sew. If your sewing machine has a free arm, use this when sewing the neck opening.

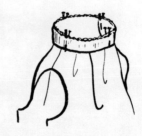

V Neck

The point of V can be finished in different ways.
Here are two of the most popular finishes.

Vertical V   Overlap V

The same procedure can be followed for both
of these variations, up to finishing the neckband
at center front.

Instead of stay stitching the point of V to keep
fabric from stretching, place "Scotch" Magic
Transparent Tape ½″ (1¼ cm.) from edge.

If you are using a Sew-Knit-N-Stretch pattern,
cut out the pattern piece for neckband either
across the grain or with the grain.*If you are using
another pattern, cut a length of fabric
approximately 26″ (66 cm.) for ladies, 29″ (74 cm.)
for men, and 2½″ (6 cm.) wide.

Fold and press band double lengthwise, wrong
sides together. Mark as indicated on pattern
piece. Pin neckband to neck opening on right
side, raw edges together, matching center
back, front shoulder seams and point of V.
The ends of neckband will extend approximately
1½″ (4 cm.) beyond point of V.

If you are not using a Sew-Knit-N-Stretch
pattern, remember to stretch the neckband
more in the back between shoulder seams
than in the front.

Be sure to match front shoulder seam as
indicated on pattern piece to get the right stretch
in the back if you are using the Sew-Knit-N-
Stretch pattern for raglan sleeves.

*Note: If you prefer a deeper V, cut the neckband
slightly longer.

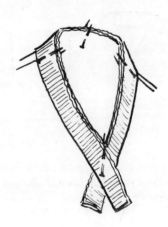

Finish for Vertical V

Begin sewing ⅛″ (2 mm.) from point of V.
Continue sewing all around to point of V on
other side.

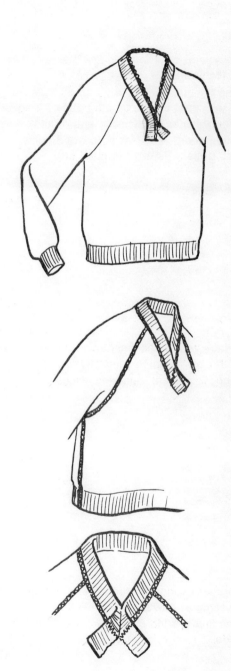

Take ends of neckband and baste
them together on wrong side to form the
point of V, as shown in diagram.

Check so the V is perfectly
vertical before final sewing. Press seam
open; sew ends to seam; trim off excess.

Finish for Overlap V

Begin sewing at distance from point of V equal
to width of neckband, leaving end of neckband
extending about 1½″ (4 cm.) beyond point of V.
Sew all around the neck to point of V.

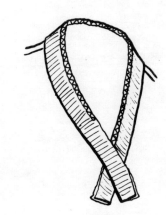

Now place end of neckband over the first tab and
insert through opening originally left.
Sew ends to point of V and trim excess.

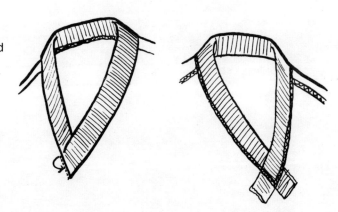

The proper overlap for this type of V neck finish
is the same as how a cardigan is buttoned,
i.e., the man's V top overlap would come from the
left side.

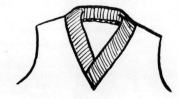

If you are making a pullover with set-in sleeves, it is easier to sew the sleeves in place before you sew the side seams. Note: the left and right sleeves in this style sweater are identical. Match center top of sleeve to shoulder seam.

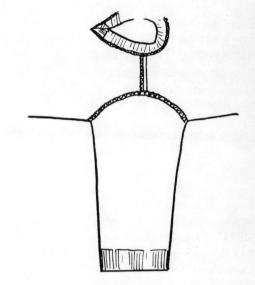

Now that your neck finish is completed, you can finish sewing the sweater. Sew the side seams and sleeve seams in one continuous operation, starting at the bottom of side seams and ending at end of sleeves.

At this point you should try your sweater on. If you find your sleeves are too wide, simply sew another seam to narrow the sleeves and cut off excess.

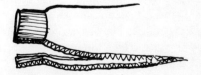

There are different ways to finish the sleeves. You may wish to sew the sleeve seam right down to the end of the cuff.

You may want a turned-up cuff. For this, sew the sleeve seam to about 1″ of where the ribbing starts. Now finish seam on the right side of fabric and the turned-up cuff will show no seam allowance.

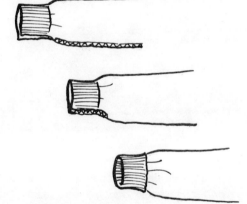

To get a professional-looking cuff, eliminate part of seam allowance from showing by sewing a few stitches by hand at end of cuff seam. This will just take a minute to do. You could also do this at bottom of side seams.

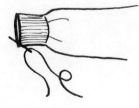

If you are using separate cuffs to finish the sleeve, divide the sleeve edges and the cuffs in fourths with pins. Sew cuffs to sleeves, matching the pins, right sides and raw edges together; stretch the cuffs to fit the sleeve openings.

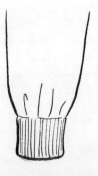

If you want a larger neck opening so you don't
ruin your hair when putting the sweater on,
you can easily insert a zipper in center back.
Refer to Chapter 8 for complete, easy-to-follow
instructions.

If you are making a round-neck pullover for a
very small child, you could also put a zipper
on the shoulder seam, or buttons and button loops.
See Chapter 10.

You may want to make a belt for your pullover.
This is very attractive made out of the same fabric
as your pullover, or in a contrasting color
(perhaps to match the neckband). The belt can be
placed at the waistline or lower. A belt about
1½″ (3½ cm.) wide finished would be
proportionately correct. You may make belt loops
(see Chapter 10), and fasten the belt with an
attractive buckle or pretty buttons.
When making a belt in sweater fabric, cut it
across the grain or use ribbing which works
beautifully.

If you are making a pullover in cotton knit or sweater yardage where you don't have a finished edge, you can either fold the fabric to wrong side and hem, or you may want to use a straight piece of fabric, fold it double (wrong sides together), and sew on bottom of sweater (right sides and raw edges together). Use this same procedure for cuffs and neckband.

You might enjoy making yarn decorations for your sweater. See Chapter 9. Here you can display your creative talents and add your own personal touch to the garment.

Personal Notes — Pullover Sweaters

_____

_____

_____

_____

_____

_____

_____

_____

_____

_____

_____

_____

_____

_____

_____

The following technics apply to making
cardigans for men, women and children.

Follow the cutting procedure outlined in
Chapter 2.

Sew the shoulder seams first.

On a man's cardigan with set-in sleeves, sew
non-stretch seam binding in shoulder seams to
prevent stretching.

For a professional touch to shoulder seams, top stitch on right side about ⅛″ (2 mm.) from seam (seam allowance turned to the back).

For set-in sleeves, attach the sleeves by matching center top of sleeve to shoulder seam.

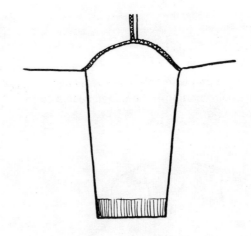

Sew side seam and sleeve seam in one continuous operation starting at bottom of side seam, finishing at end of sleeve.

Neckband for Ladies' and Girls' Cardigan

For the neckband, cut a straight piece of fabric or ribbing across the grain, 2″ (5 cm.) wide or as wide as desired. The stretch factor in fabric varies, but a 16″ (40 cm.) length will be more than enough for any neckband. To get correct size for neckband, stretch band around neck so it feels comfortable and cut off excess.

Fold and press neckband double lengthwise, wrong sides together. Divide neckband and neck opening of sweater in fourths with pins. Pin neckband to right side of neck opening, raw edges together, matching the pins. Sew on band, stretching it to fit neck opening.

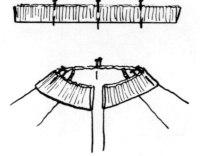

Front Finish for Ladies' and Girls' Cardigan Using Grosgrain Ribbon

Use ¾″ (2 cm.) wide grosgrain ribbon. Cut two lengths of grosgrain ribbon long enough for front of sweater and extending ½″ (1¼ cm.) over top and bottom. You may want to have it showing as a decoration in the front or turned to the back to make a firm facing for buttons and buttonholes.

If you want to use it as a firm facing, place the ribbon on right side of fronts by overlapping ¼″ (6 mm.). If you want it as a decoration on the front, place the ribbon on the wrong side, overlapping ¼″ (6 mm.).

Sew ribbon to sweater with a straight stitch close to ribbon edge.

If you are using it as a decoration, turn ribbon to right side and make a top stitch close to the other ribbon edge to hold it in place.

If you're using it as a facing, turn ribbon to wrong side and it will be held in place with buttons and buttonholes.

No matter how you are using the ribbon, turn top and bottom ends under ½″ (1¼ cm.) and hand stitch to finish.

Front Finish for Ladies' and Girls' Cardigan Using Sweater Fabric

Cut two straight pieces of fabric along or across the grain. The length of each piece of fabric is equal to front of sweater plus 1″ (2½ cm.) — ½″ (1¼ cm.) will extend beyond top and bottom. The approximate width is 2½″ (6 cm.). Fold and press band lengthwise, wrong sides together.

After pressing, check the length with sweater front. The bands may have stretched slightly during pressing and if so, cut off the excess.

Sew bands on sweater fronts, right sides and raw edges together, leaving ½″ (1¼ cm.) extending over top and bottom. Finish ends of bands by tucking in ½″ (1¼ cm.) and hand stitch to finish. Turn and press.

**Neckband and Front Finish for Men's and Boys'
Cardigan Using Rolled Edge Trim**

Cut length of trim long enough to go around
left front, neck opening and right front plus
extending ½″ (1¼ cm.) on both sides. Pin trim to
sweater by overlapping the rolled edge portion
½″ (1¼ cm.) on right side of fabric. The trim
has to be stretched between the back shoulder
seams approximately 1½″ (3½ cm.) for men,
¾″ (2 cm.) for boys.

Sew ¼″ (6 mm.) from rolled edge of trim.
Turn trim to wrong side so only the rolled edge
portion is showing from right side.

Buttons and buttonholes will hold the trim in place
on the fronts. Sew a few stitches by hand to
hold trim in place between the back shoulder
seams.

Finish trim at bottom of cardigan by turning
½″ (1¼ cm.) to wrong side to form a hem.
Hand stitch to finish.

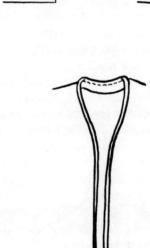

Neckband and Front Finish for Men's and Boys' Cardigan Using Sweater Fabric

Cut a piece of fabric either across or along the grain, long enough to go around left front, neck opening and right front and extending ½″ (1¼ cm.) on both sides. Width of band for men is 2½″ (6½ cm.); for boys, 2″ (5 cm.).

Press band double lengthwise, wrong sides together.

Pin band to sweater, right sides and raw edges together. For men the band has to be stretched between the shoulder seams approximately 1½″ (3½ cm.) and from shoulder seams to point of V, approximately ½″ (1¼ cm.); then continue sewing without stretching the band. For boys' cardigans, stretch the band ¾″ (2 cm.) between shoulder seams and ½″ (6 mm.) from shoulder seams to point of V; then continue sewing without stretching the band.

Finish bands at bottom of cardigan by tucking in ½″ (1¼ cm.). Hand stitch to finish.

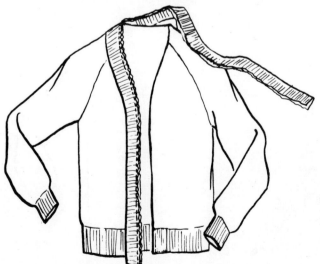

Buttons and Buttonholes

When making buttonholes, remember that men's and boys' go on the left side — ladies' and girls' on the right.

In making a ladies' or girls' cardigan, the top buttonhole is horizontal and the rest are vertical.

Men's and boys' buttonholes are almost always vertical.

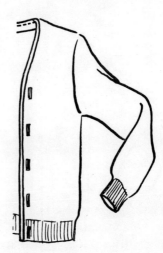

You can make buttonholes in sweater fabric
either by hand or with a sewing machine. If you
are making the buttonholes on your sewing
machine, use "Scotch" Magic Transparent Tape
to prevent fabric from catching in the presser foot.

Place the tape where the buttonholes will be
sewn on the right side of fabric. You can mark on
the tape the positions of the buttonholes
(but use a pencil as a ballpoint pen may leave
marks on the fabric).

When sewing buttonholes in knit and stretch
fabric, you should always use slightly longer
stitch length on your sewing machine. If possible
make a corded buttonhole because it will be
sturdier and will not ripple. Refer to your
sewing machine instruction book for making a
corded buttonhole.

The buttons, of course, can be sewn on by hand,
but the easiest way, if you have a zigzag
machine, is to drop the feed dog and use a
zigzag stitch as wide as the holes in the button.
Here again we recommend placing tape where
buttons will be sewn. It will prevent the fabric from
pulling up into the holes of the button.

If you want a shank to the buttons, we suggest
you use a button reed which is available from
Viking (Husqvarna) sewing machine dealers.

Sweater Jacket

Instead of buttons and buttonholes for a front finish, you could use a zipper. An attractive way to use a zipper is to have a wide neckband (such as a mock turtleneck) and sew the zipper all the way up to the top.

Be sure to use a separating zipper, one that comes in two pieces and is not connected at the bottom.

Vest

Using Sweater Fabric

If you would like to make a vest in sweater fabric, we suggest you use a sweater pattern with set-in sleeves.

Follow pattern instructions, omitting the sleeves. Finish the sleeve opening by cutting a straight piece of fabric as wide as desired and long enough to go around sleeve opening. Sew ends together to form a circle. Fold double lengthwise, wrong sides together. Divide bands and sleeve openings in fourths with pins and sew on, right side to right side, raw edges together.

Sweater Pocket

This technic can be used for any size pocket
you desire. The measurements we use to describe
the procedure will result in a finished pocket welt
of 4″ x ¾″ (10 cm. x 2 cm.).

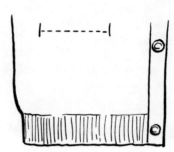

1. Decide where you want your pocket and
   mark with chalk.

2. Cut a piece of fabric 6″ (15 cm.) long and
   2″ (5 cm.) wide for pocket welt.

3. Press welt double lengthwise, wrong sides
   together.

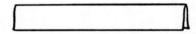

4. Cut pieces of sweater fabric and pocket lining
   6″ x 6″ (15 cm. x 15 cm.).

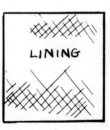

5. Place welt, open edges up, directly under
   chalk line for pocket with 1″ (2½ cm.)
   extending on each side. Tape ends in place.

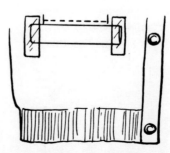

6. Place 6″ x 6″ (15 cm. x 15 cm.) piece of sweater fabric directly above taped welt. Tape in place.

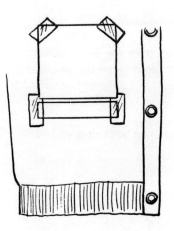

7. Place 6″ x 6″ (15 cm. x 15 cm.) piece of lining on top of welt. Pin in place.

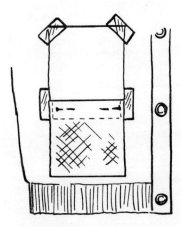

8. Place pieces of tape on ends of lining and sweater fabric to indicate width of pocket 4″ (10 cm.).

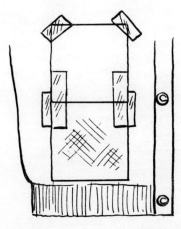

9. Place a strip of tape about ¼″ (6 mm.) down from top edge of lining. Measure exactly ¾″ (2 cm.) from top edge of this piece of tape and mark with another piece of tape.

The area inside the tape should now be 4″ x ¾″ (10 cm. x 2 cm.) or the size of the finished welt.

10. Using the tape as a guide, sew a seam all the way around this 4″ x ¾″ (10 cm. x 2 cm.) opening. Sew at edge of tape — not through it. If you are using a Viking sewing machine, use the elastic straightstitch; otherwise use a plain straight stitch.

11. Remove all tape and pins.
Turn over to wrong side. Cut an opening in the middle of sewn area, ½″ (1¼ cm.) from each end.

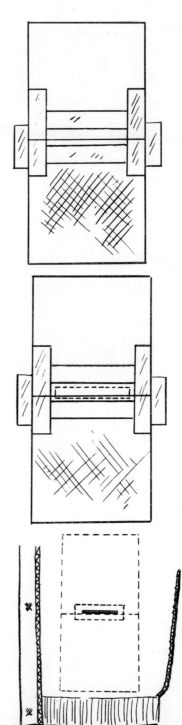

12. From this opening, cut angles to each corner.

13. On long sides of opening, trim seam allowances to ¼″ (6 mm.) Overcast edges of long sides. Leave end tabs free.

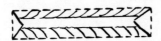

14. Turn lining and sweater fabric to wrong side through opening. Sweater fabric and lining are facing down.

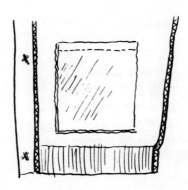

15. Turn ends of welt to wrong side through opening.

Your welt should now completely cover the opening.

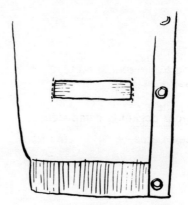

16. On wrong side, place a pin at each end of welt, on the small triangles and exactly on the seam.

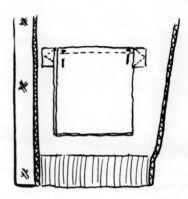

17. Pin lining and fabric together and mark on lining the shape you want your pocket to be.

   Begin sewing at pin (on welt and small triangle) precisely on the seam. Sew completely around the pocket shape you have marked on lining, ending up at other pin. Use Blue-Blue-Blue setting for Viking (Husqvarna) sewing machines.

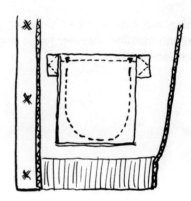

18. Trim excess leaving ¼″ (6 mm.) seam allowance. Overcast the edges.

   Steam press and your pocket is completed.

Personal Notes — Cardigan Sweater

This chapter covers two technics for making skirts. One technic is for knit and stretch fabric; the other applies to sweater fabric.

Straight Skirt

Using Knit and Stretch Fabric

A zipper is not needed in this skirt unless you have a very small waist in proportion to your hips.

Before cutting, check your measurements with the pattern. Cut out the pattern pieces on the grain of fabric with the exception of the waistband which is cut across the grain. The greatest stretch of the material should go *around* the body — otherwise you may end up with a skirt that stretches lengthwise.

The proper length of waistband is your waist measurement plus 1″ (2½ cm.). The width of the waistband will depend on the width of the elastic you are using. We recommend using ¾″ or 1″ (2 or 2½ cm.) wide elastic. For 1″ (2½ cm.) wide elastic, you would cut your waistband 2½″ (6½ cm.) wide.

Sew the darts first. Darts are much easier to make before you have sewn the side seams. (Correct way to press darts is toward the center).

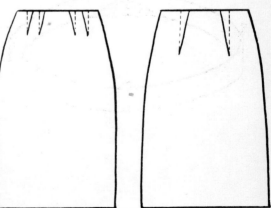

Now sew the side seams and press seams open.

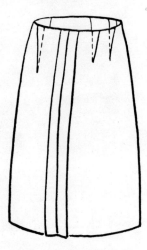

Measure elastic using your exact waist measurement plus enough extra for seam allowance. Sew ends securely together to form a circle.

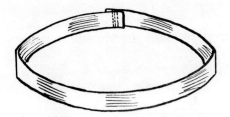

Pin elastic close to the fold inside waistband.

Sew ends of waistband together to form a circle using ⅝″ (1½ cm.) seam allowance. Press seam open. Press waistband double lengthwise with wrong sides together. At this point check to make sure waistband slips easily over your hips. Divide waistband in fourths with pins.

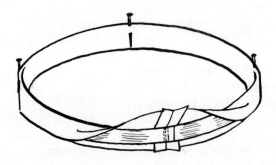

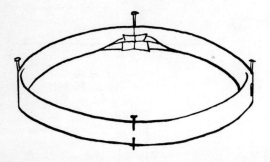

Divide waist opening in skirt in fourths with pins.

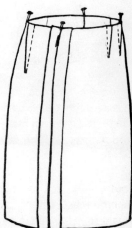

Match the pins and sew waistband to skirt in
one operation, right sides and raw edges together.
The elastic is now sewn inside the waistband.

Hem skirt to desired length. See Chapter 1.

Straight Skirt

Using Sweater Fabric

This technic was designed for making a skirt with a sweater body, sweater blanket or sweater yardage. It's not necessary to have darts, zipper or separate waistband when using this type of fabric.

Before cutting out the pattern pieces, check your hip measurement to be sure it agrees with the pattern. Also be sure you cut your skirt on the proper grain of fabric. If your sweater fabric has a ribbed finish, you can place this ribbing at the bottom of the skirt instead of a hem (if the ribbing is narrow), or you can use the ribbing at the waistband to be sewn into a casing.

Sew-Knit-N-Stretch patterns include ¼″ (6 mm.) seam allowance. If you prefer to press the seams open, be sure to add more seam allowance.

Sew the side seams and press. See Chapter 1.

When sewing ¼″ (6 mm.) seam allowance on side seams with zigzag or Viking (Husqvarna) sewing machines, before sewing the seams, place strips of "Scotch" Magic Transparent Tape ½″ (1¼ cm.) from edge of fabric to avoid rippling.

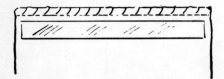

To finish the waistband, simply fold top of skirt over to wrong side to form a casing for the elastic. If you are using ¾″ (2 cm.) wide elastic, fold the top over 1″ (2½ cm.). The easiest way to finish your waistband is to measure elastic around your waist so it feels comfortable and sew the ends securely to form a circle. Then just place the circle of elastic inside casing and make your casing seam.

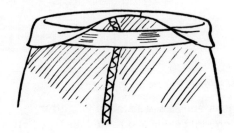

If you wish to sew the casing first (and then insert the elastic), do not sew elastic together to form a circle and be sure to leave a 1″ (2½ cm.) opening to thread the elastic.

Hem to desired length. See Chapter 1.

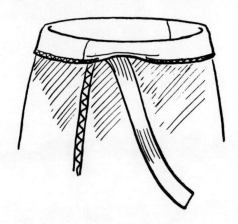

Personal Notes — Ladies' Skirts

Ladies' Slacks

It's difficult to buy a pair of slacks that fit
exactly as you like.

The legs may be too wide, too narrow, or even
too short. Slacks are very easy to sew with knit
and stretch fabric, and you can make them fit
to your individual taste. With knit and stretch
fabric it is not necessary to use a zipper.

There is one basic technic that we recommend
for making slacks, up to the waistband, for
which we have two simple variations. One technic
utilizes a separate waistband; the other involves
merely folding the top of your slacks over to
form a casing for the elastic.

Basic Technic

Before cutting, check your measurements with
the pattern for correct size and proper length.
Measure your hip at largest point and add
approximately 1″ (2½ cm.) for freedom
of movement.

Place fabric right sides together. Be very sure
to place your pattern pieces exactly on the grain
of fabric. This is extremely important with
regard to creases. Also, if your pieces are not
exactly straight, you may end up with more
stretch in one leg.

Sew-Knit-N-Stretch patterns include ¼″ (6 mm.)
seam allowance; however, if you want to press
the seam open, be sure to add extra allowance.

If you are not using a Sew-Knit-N-Stretch pattern,
and if you are not using a separate waistband,
add extra fabric at top of slacks for waistband
casing.

Cuffs require extra fabric at bottom of legs, so
be sure to plan accordingly before you cut.

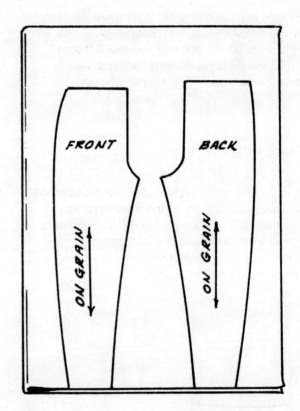

As soon as you have cut out your pattern pieces (and while the two backs are lying together, etc.), pin the crotch seams and sew them. We recommend doing this because the four pattern pieces are very similar and can become mixed up. After you sew the crotch seams, however, you then have only the back and front pieces to work with.

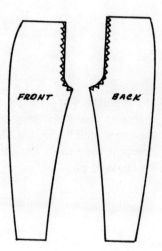

Sew the outside seams and press them. (They are easier to press before the inside seams are sewn.)

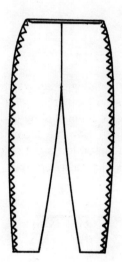

Sew the inside leg seams by starting at bottom of one leg and sewing continuously to bottom of other leg.

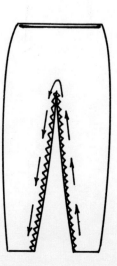

Now it's time to fit the slacks. Put them on and
tie a string snugly around your waist (over the
slacks). Pull the slacks up until the crotch fits
properly, even when you bend over. Mark the
string position with chalk or pins.

If you have a proportionately small waistline and
want to avoid a gathered look around the waist,
you can pin in the back seam slightly (side
seams too, if necessary). Sew the seams and cut
off excess fabric — no need to rip out stitches.
Make sure the slacks slip easily up over
your hips.

Folded Waistband

We recommend using ¾″ (2 cm.) wide elastic.
For this width elastic, measure 1¼″ (3 cm.) from
string position and cut off excess.

Fold fabric to wrong side at string position to
form a casing.

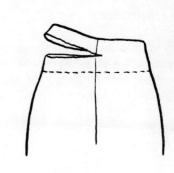

Now measure elastic around your waist so it
feels comfortable and sew the ends securely
together to form a circle.

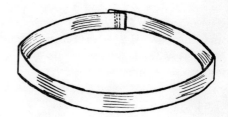

Place elastic inside the casing as you sew the
casing seam.

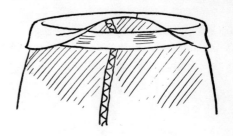

If you prefer, you can sew the casing first, leaving
a 1″ (2½ cm.) opening for threading the elastic.
Pull the correct length of elastic through casing
and sew ends securely together.

Separate Waistband

You may wish to make darts or taper the side seams depending on how you want your slacks to fit. Just be sure the slacks still slip easily over your hips before sewing on the waistband.

Measure ¼″ (6 mm.) from string position and cut off excess.

Cut a straight piece of fabric across the grain. Proper length for waistband is your waist measurement plus 2″ (5 cm.). The correct width for the waistband is 2″ (5 cm.) if you are using ¾″ (2 cm.) wide elastic. Sew ends together to form a circle using ⅝″ (1½ cm.) seam allowance. Be sure this circle slips easily over hips.

Press waistband double lengthwise, wrong sides together.

Measure elastic comfortably around your waist and sew ends securely to form a circle. Divide waistband and waist opening in fourths with pins.

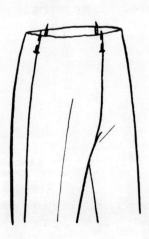

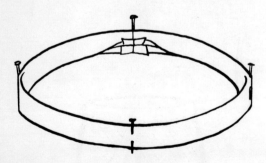

Place circle of elastic inside waistband. Sew
waistband to slacks, right sides and raw edges
together, by matching the pins. (Waistband can be
stretched to fit waist opening.)

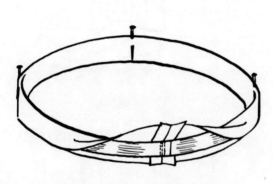
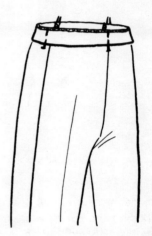

If you get a few puckers around the waistband,
these can usually be eliminated by steam
pressing.

Now try the slacks on. Here is where you will
really appreciate the wonderful stretch factor of
this fabric. Notice how your slacks fit smoothly
and comfortably around your hips and waistline
with no unnecessary fullness which is so
unflattering in slacks.

Mark your hemline with pins or chalk. If you are
not making cuffs on your slacks, turn hem to
wrong side and finish either by hand or by
elastic blindstitch, which is invisible from right
side of fabric. See Chapter 1 for hemming
technic.

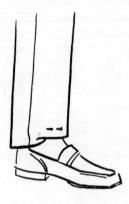

Cuffs

From hemline, measure twice desired cuff length
plus ¾″ (2 cm.) and cut off excess. Now measure
down from hemline width of desired cuff, fold
to wrong side and press. Sew a seam on fabric
edge using ¼″ (6 mm.) seam allowance.
This seam will be slightly above your hemline.
If you have a free arm on your sewing machine,
use it to sew this seam.

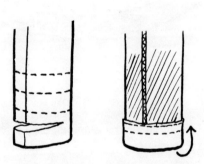

Fold up cuff to right side and press.

Secure cuff to slacks by folding top edge of cuff down approximately ¼″ (6 mm.) and tack in about four places.

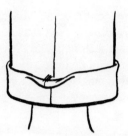

Separate Cuffs

If you are short of yardage and still want cuffs on your slacks, leave only ¼″ (6 mm.) hem allowance at bottom of slacks. Make separate cuffs by cutting straight piece of fabric as wide as desired and long enough to go around bottom of slacks plus seam allowance.

Sew ends of cuffs together to form circles to fit bottom of slacks. Be sure your measurements are precise.

Press cuffs double lengthwise, wrong sides together.

Sew cuffs to bottom of slacks by placing cuffs on wrong side, raw edges together. Turn up cuffs and press. Secure cuffs to slacks by tacking as described above.

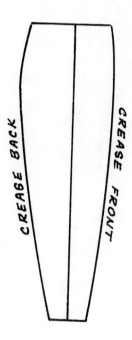

Press slacks by matching outside seam to inside seam and pressing all the way up.

If you want permanent creases, you can sew a seam on the very edge of the creases. This can be done with an elastic straightstitch if your sewing machine has it, or you can use a double needle, making a raised seam. However, never use cord inside your raised seams in knit and stretch fabric.

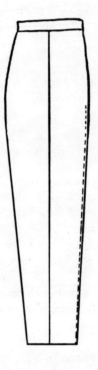

Ladies' Ski Pants

Ski pants are worn by skiers and "spectators"
alike — the spectators being those hardy
individuals who think it's just as much fun to
socialize around the fireplace as it is to
"schuss" a slope.

It's not difficult at all to sew your own ski pants
and there are many reasons why you should.
By sewing your own ski pants, you will get a
custom fit which is so important in this type of
garment. You will have ski pants that do not bag
in the legs (so unflattering); you will obtain the
correct crotch fit so your bending and jumping
will not be restricted, and you will get the stretch
of the fabric where you need it most. If these
are not enough advantages why you should sew
your own ski pants, the money you will save
certainly should persuade you.

When you sew ski pants, it is extremely important
to use a stitch that will stretch with the fabric.
Refer to Chapter 1 for proper seams to use.
Remember to use normal pressure on presser
foot and normal thread tension.

You may use one-way or two-way stretch fabric
for your ski pants. Just make sure that the
greater stretch of fabric goes up and down
(vertically) to allow freedom of motion for knee
bends, jumping, etc. However, the waistband
should be cut with the stretch going around the
body. Use whatever weight of fabric you desire.
The heavier fabric naturally will be warmer
while a lighter weight fabric is more comfortable
for after-ski wear.

Be sure to check your measurements with the
pattern before cutting. You should allow enough
room for freedom of movement plus room for
the heavier undergarments you will be wearing.
Also check the length of the legs — they should be
slightly shorter than your actual leg measurement
since they will stretch up and down. If necessary,
the length of the legs can be adjusted, even
after the ski pants are made, by shortening them
at the hem. Check your waist measurement and
allow for the button and buttonhole tab.

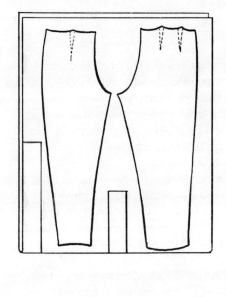

Fold the fabric double, right sides together.
Be sure to check the arrows on the pattern pieces
to get proper stretch of fabric. Ski pants have
two darts on each back piece; one dart on each
front piece. The reason for this is to allow more
fullness in the back. Mark the darts with
chalk or pins.

Sew center front seam and center back seam
first, using narrow seam allowance.

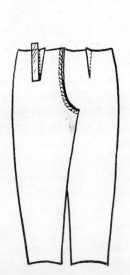

Then sew darts and press toward center.

Now you have just one front piece and one back piece. Proceed to sew the side seams using ⅝″ (1½ cm.) seam allowance. Be sure to leave an opening in left side seam for zipper insertion. Baste the zipper opening with a long straight stitch and loose thread tension. Press the seam allowance open and remove basting on zipper opening.

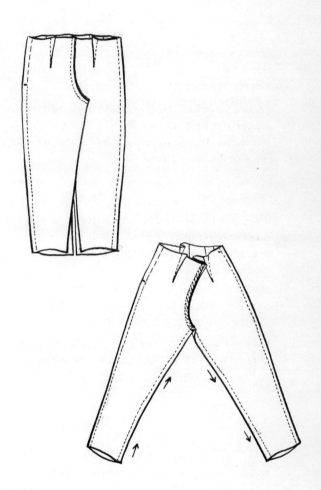

Next sew the inside leg seam in one continuous operation (from bottom of one leg to bottom of the other). Stretch the back piece slightly as you sew the top thigh area.

Try the ski pants on at this point and fit the crotch. See Chapter 1, Fitting. Mark your exact waist position (after bending over) and allow ¼″ (6 mm.) for seam allowance. Cut off excess.

Now is the easiest time to insert the zipper. We recommend using a good quality metal zipper that is able to withstand extra stress. Use the technic outlined in Chapter 8 or tape the zipper in place on wrong side of opening, then top stitch on right side through fabric and cloth edge of zipper, using the same width seam allowance on both edges. This latter technic holds the zipper more securely and is therefore recommended.

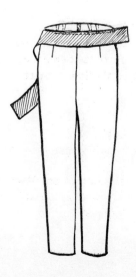

Attach the waistband to ski pants by placing right side of waistband to right side of waist opening, raw edges together, with the waistband tab for buttonhole extended on front of slacks. Sew the waistband to waist opening using ¼″ (6 mm.) seam allowance.

You may use skirt belting inside the waistband or rubberized belting such as Stay-lastic. We recommend rubberized belting because it holds the waistband in place better.

If you use rubberized belting, it goes around your waist only — not on the buttonhole tab. Sew it to the right side (top half) of the waistband, rubber side out.

Fold the ends of belting in ¼" (6 mm.) and top stitch. Then trim the fabric under belting to eliminate bulkiness.

If you prefer skirt belting in the waistband, sew this on the wrong side of bottom half of waistband. Again, do not insert this stiffness in the buttonhole tab.

Finish the buttonhole tab by folding waistband double lengthwise, the width of the belting. Sew a seam on two unsewn edges starting at exact point of zipper.

Then turn the tab to right side and press. Sew up the other end of waistband (where button will be sewn) in exact line with zipper. Turn to right side.

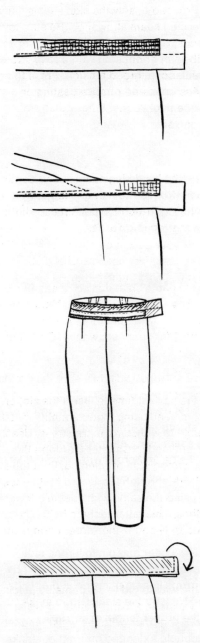

The waistband is now turned to wrong side of waist opening with seam allowance in waistband. Sew waistband in place from right side of ski pants as close as possible to first waistband seam. Be sure your stitches catch waistband on wrong side.

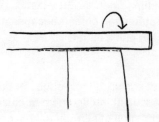

Now you can make the buttonhole (horizontally) on the buttonhole tab. Then close the zipper and sew your button on the other side. If you have a zigzag machine, use this to sew your button on as it will hold much better.

Cut two stirrups and make sure the greater stretch of fabric goes lengthwise. Your stirrups can be as narrow or as wide as you wish. Fold each stirrup lengthwise, right sides together, and sew a seam using narrow seam allowance. Turn to right side and press with seam centered.

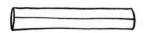

Fold hem under and pin to wrong side. Recommended hem allowance is 1″ (2½ cm.). Pin stirrups to hem at inside and outside leg seams. Now try the slacks on to make sure you have the proper length of stirrup.

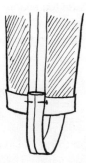

Trim the ends of stirrups at raw edges of hem.
Overcast raw edges all around hem (including
stirrups). Secure ends of stirrups to hem **only**
(one thickness) with a seam approximately ½"
(1¼" cm.) from stirrup ends, and hem bottom
of slacks.

To reinforce stirrups, sew a seam from right
side exactly on inside and outside leg seams,
through stirrup ends.

To get the proper press creases in ski pants, line
up inside and outside leg seams and steam press.

Personal Notes — Ladies' Slacks and Ski Pants

_____   _____

_____   _____

_____   _____

_____   _____

_____   _____

_____   _____

_____   _____

_____   _____

_____   _____

_____   _____

_____   _____

_____   _____

_____   _____

_____   _____

_____   _____

The shell is a very important part of your wardrobe. This garment is extremely versatile — it can be worn with a skirt, slacks, suits — and can add interest to an otherwise ordinary ensemble. It can be made from a small amount of fabric and with our new technic, it's one of the easiest garments to make.

Shells can have a wide variety of neck finishes — from narrow neckbands to turtlenecks — and the sewing technic is the same for all. You can add a belt to your shell in the same fabric or perhaps in a co-ordinating color. Your shell can be as long as you wish and can be easily extended to a dress by making it a little wider over the hips.

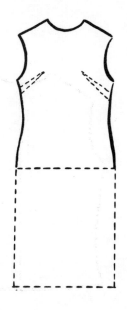

The dart positions can be changed to wherever
you feel they look best. Just fold the darts on
the pattern piece and tape in place. Now the
pattern piece will protrude representing dart
fullness. Decide where you want your darts to
begin and cut straight to point of the folded, taped
darts. Your pattern piece will now lie flat again
and you will have the same size darts, but
in the positions you prefer.

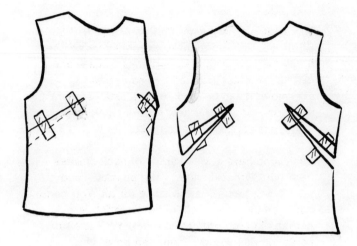

Before cutting your shell, check your
measurements with pattern to get correct size
and length of body. The width of neck and arm
bands may be cut to your specifications,
depending on what style you prefer.

Cut out your pattern pieces. If you are making
a shell with a seam in center back, sew this seam
first and if you are using a zipper, insert it now.

Sew and press darts. Press side seam darts
down; vertical darts should be pressed toward
the center.

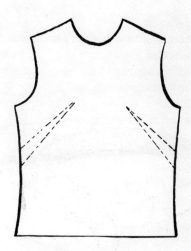

Sew shoulder seams and side seams. When
using ¼″ (6 mm.) seam allowance, press the
seams towards the back; for ⅝″ (1½ cm.) seam
allowance, press seams open.

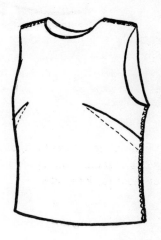

If you are using a Sew-Knit-N-Stretch pattern,
you have a pattern piece for the neckband and
armbands. However, if you are not using this
pattern and have no pattern piece to go by,
cut three pieces approximately 16″ (40 cm.) long
and as wide as you desire. (The neckband and
armbands are all cut the same length). Make
sure these bands agree with your measurements
and if they are too large, just cut off the excess.

Sew ends of the two arm bands together to form circles.

Fold all three bands lengthwise, wrong sides together, and press. Divide the bands in fourths with pins.

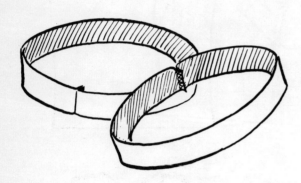

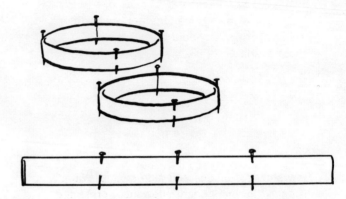

Finish ends of neckband by folding lengthwise, right sides together, and sewing the end edges. Turn corners to right side.

Divide arm and neck openings in fourths with pins.

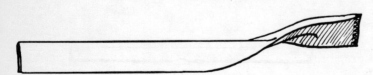

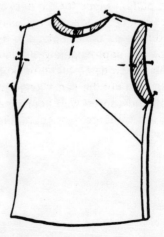

Pin arm bands to arm openings, right sides and raw edges together, by matching the pins. Sew bands on using ¼″ (6 mm.) seam allowance.

Pin and sew neckband to neck opening, right sides and raw edges together, by matching the pins. The ends should meet exactly — not overlap.

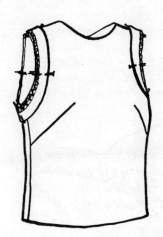

If you are using a zipper in back seam, sew a hook and eye in center back of neck band.

As a variation (and if you are not using a zipper), you could use a pretty button and button loop to fasten neckband. Just be sure your opening is large enough to go over your head.

If you want a belt, cut a piece of fabric long enough to tie around your waist, approximately 2½″ (6½ cm.) wide. Fold double, right sides together; sew around raw edges leaving a 1″ (2½ cm.) opening in the middle of belt for turning. Turn right side out; sew opening by hand and press.

Corded Belt

Cut a straight piece of fabric as long as you
want your belt to be. Cut length of cord *twice* as
long as this piece of fabric.

Fold fabric right sides together and place one-half
of the cord inside. The other half of the cord
will extend outside the fabric. Sew a few stitches
at half-way mark of cord, securing the cord
to fabric at that point.

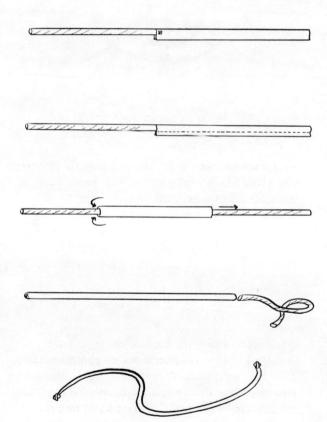

Now sew a seam as close to cord as possible
(without catching the cord with stitches).

Pull the top end of cord sewn in the fabric.
The fabric will turn as you pull, covering the other
half of the cord with fabric, right side out.

Cut off cord ends about ¼″ (6 mm.) shorter than
the fabric. Tuck in fabric and finish by sewing
a few stitches by hand.

For an extra touch, tie a knot at each end of
your belt.

Personal Notes — Ladies' Shells

_____

_____

_____

_____

_____

_____

_____

_____

_____

_____

_____

_____

_____

_____

A swimsuit is one of the easiest garments to sew. Thanks to the wonderful stretch factor of the fabric, fitting need not be a problem. Now you can have several swimsuits for the price you normally would pay for one.

The fabric we recommend is two-way stretch swimsuit fabric. This fabric stretches more one way than the other, so be sure the greater stretch goes *around* the body. The fabric, lining, bra cups, and elastic used should be able to retain their shape in water. Swimsuit fabric, especially the lighter colors, may have to be laundered. It is not unusual to find spots on the swimsuit fabric you buy and laundering the fabric is, in fact, a procedure generally followed by the swimsuit manufacturers themselves.

You should use a pattern designed specifically for two-way stretch swimsuit fabric. The patterns referred to in this chapter are SEW-KNIT-N-STRETCH patterns. These patterns are designed for swimsuit fabric with medium stretch. Therefore, if your fabric has more than medium stretch, use a smaller size pattern. If it has a lower stretch factor, use a larger size.

It is usually not necessary to alter your swimsuit pattern to obtain the proper fit. However, here is an example of how the bustline could be altered by increasing or decreasing the bust on the side panels.

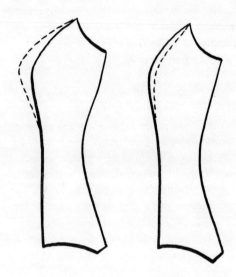

If you increase the bustline on the side panels, increase the front pattern piece accordingly by lengthening it using separate paper insert. If you minimize the bustline, shorten the front pattern piece by folding it.

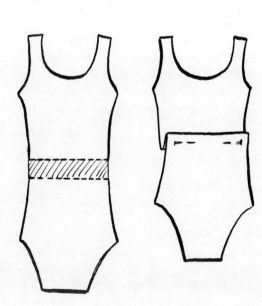

Place fabric right sides together and arrange pattern pieces on grain of fabric, following the arrows. Use pins or heavy weights to hold pattern pieces to fabric. Always be sure to use sharp pins, sewing needles and scissors as the elastic thread in the fabric makes it sturdier than other fabric. Before cutting, be absolutely sure the pieces lie on the proper grain of fabric so that the greater stretch goes around the body. This is essential for proper fitting.

Some swimsuit fabric is heavier than others and does not require lining except for the crotch, which always should be lined. If your swimsuit fabric is lightweight, line the entire swimsuit with lightweight lining made for swimsuits. This type of lining has a greater stretch factor than the swimsuit. Cut out the lining at the same time you cut the swimsuit fabric. You can sew two separate swimsuits — one of lining, one of swimsuit fabric but we recommend sewing the lining into the seams as you assemble your swimsuit. This method is much easier and faster and makes a more professional looking garment. In a swimsuit with separate lining, the lining seams may show through when the suit is wet.

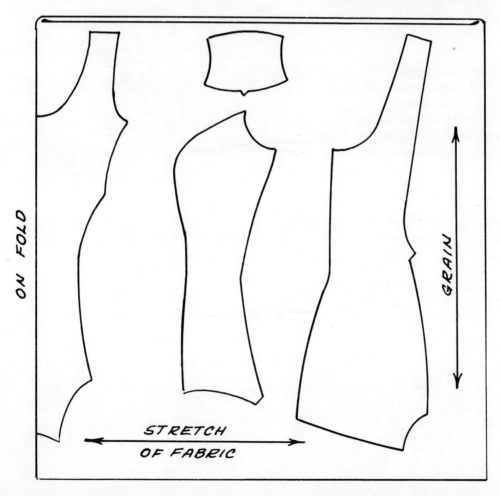

You can sew a swimsuit with any sewing machine. Some brands are more suitable and easier to use than others. To get the best results when sewing with any kind of sewing machine, use normal pressure on the presser foot and a fine sewing machine needle. Also, this fabric is much easier to sew if you use a roller presser foot.

The best seam to use is very similar to seams on ready-made swimsuits. This seam is elastic (called the serging-type seam), and it sews the pieces together and overcasts in one operation. This seam can be made on a Viking (Husqvarna) sewing machine.

If your sewing machine has a zigzag stitch, use this rather than a straight stitch to sew the seams. Set the stitch length at medium and the zigzag control at slightly narrower than medium width. This seam will be elastic. If fabric requires overcasting, use the largest zigzag stitch.

If you have a straight stitch sewing machine, be sure to stretch the fabric in back as well as in front of the presser foot as you are sewing. Set the stitch length at medium and sew the seam two or three times, close together, for a strong seam. Overcast seam allowances together by hand.

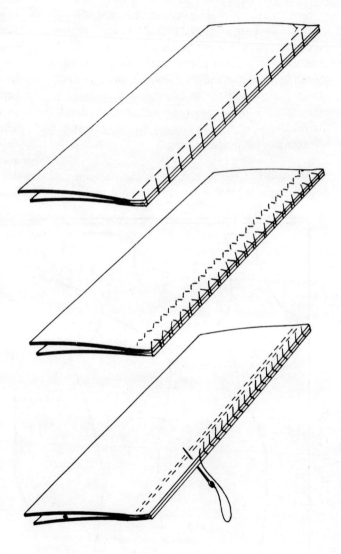

Ladies One-Piece Swimsuit

One-piece swimsuits may be the easiest for you
to start with, also the fastest.

After you have cut out your pattern pieces, pick
up the back pieces, leaving right sides together,
and sew center back seam. Now sew the front
side seams. If you are using a Sew-Knit-N-Stretch
pattern, match the notches to get a smooth
curve on the bustline. You now have just the
back and front to work with and there is no
chance of mixing up the pattern pieces.

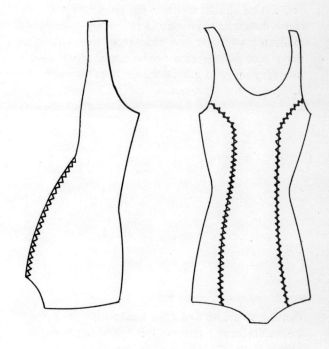

Next sew the crotch, attaching lining at the same
time. Sew the crotch piece to the back of
swimsuit first — it's easier to sew this curvey
seam before the front crotch seam is sewn.
Place the crotch piece on top of the back piece
(it will be easier to follow the curve) and sew
your seam. Then go ahead and sew the
front crotch seam.

Sew the side seams and try on the swimsuit.
Never try the swimsuit on wrong side out because
your left and right sides are not exactly the same.

When you have the swimsuit on (right side out) you will be able to feel how the stretch factor forms the fabric to your body. However, if you have made the swimsuit in a size larger than you need, just pin the side seams accordingly, sew another seam and trim off the old one. No need to rip out the old seam.

Pull the straps up to get the right length for the swimsuit. Don't pull them too tightly because the elastic in the decolletage and arm openings will shorten them somewhat. The shoulder straps can be made shorter by using wider seam allowance.

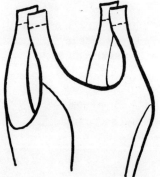

If you require longer shoulder straps, simply sew extra lengths to extend them. If you wish, conceal the insert seams with a decoration such as an applique, a bow, etc. We suggest you tape extra strips of paper on the shoulder straps of your pattern piece so your next swimsuit will be cut to your exact specifications.

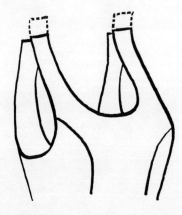

Sew the shoulder straps together and your
swimsuit is ready for the elastic. Use ⅜″ (1 cm.)
wide elastic specially treated for chlorine water.
This is very important because the elastic must
snap back into shape, even when wet. Also, it will
turn nylon yellow if it has not been treated
for chlorine.

Cut elastic lengths according to pattern
instructions, or measure elastic around leg
opening, arm openings and decolletage for proper
lengths. Sew lengths together overlapping
½″ (1¼ cm.) to form five circles. Before sewing
to swimsuit, try elastic circles around legs
and arms to make sure they feel comfortable.

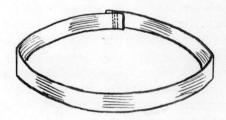

If you are lining the entire swimsuit separately,
you now have a separate swimsuit of lining.
Place the lining inside swimsuit, wrong sides
together, and sew seams around arm and leg
openings to facilitate sewing the elastic.

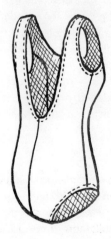

Attaching the Elastic

If you use a straight stitch sewing machine,
be sure to stretch the fabric as well as the elastic.
For zigzag sewing machines, use the largest
zigzag stitch. If you have a Viking (Husqvarna)
sewing machine, use the three-step zigzag which
consists of three small stitches in each zig
and each zag. The exceptional strength of this
seam makes it ideal for sewing on elastic.

Divide arm openings in fourths with pins; divide
elastic circles for arm openings in fourths with
pins. Pin the two elastic circles edge to edge
on wrong side. It's best to place the seam in the
elastic at some point in the back of arm opening.
By matching the pins you get the right stretch
around each opening. Sew the elastic to swimsuit,
stretching elastic slightly between the pins.

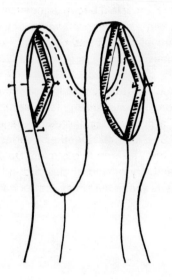

Pin elastic circles for leg openings to front of
swimsuit (on wrong side) WITHOUT stretching the
elastic. Sew elastic first to front of swimsuit
(do not stretch elastic); then sew the elastic to
back and crotch, and here you DO stretch the
elastic. This technic will give you the proper
fit around the leg openings.

Sew on elastic for decolletage by slightly
stretching elastic across center front area and
at center back.

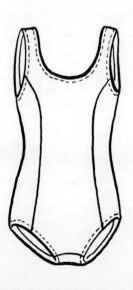

After elastic is sewn on swimsuit, turn elastic to
form hems and make a top stitch from the right
side of the garment. Use the same width of
top stitching around decolletage, arm and leg
openings for a more professional look. If you
have a straight stitch sewing machine, use longer
than normal stitch length and remember to
stretch the fabric. For a zigzag sewing machine,
use a zigzag stitch in medium width and length.
With a Viking (Husqvarna) sewing machine, use
the elastic straightstitch. This stitch moves
forward and backward three times so the seam
will be as elastic as the fabric itself.

Ladies' Swimsuit with Front Skirt

This is a very flattering style for the fuller figure.
It is also a very comfortable swimsuit and very
easy to make — you use the same technic as for
the ladies' one-piece swimsuit except here
you will make a "lining" under the skirt out of the
same fabric. This pattern is available from
SEW-KNIT-N-STRETCH, complete with
easy-to-follow instructions.

A variation you may want to try is adding a seam
at center front. You do this simply by cutting
the front piece in two, down center front, adding
for seam allowance. This gives you an extra
vertical line and is very attractive.

There are several different types of bra cups
on the market and they come in different sizes.
Be sure to use bra cups that will retain their
shape in water. The easiest to use in a swimsuit
has elastic tabs sewn on each side. With this
type you merely attach the elastic tabs into the
side seams. You may wish to sew a few stitches
by hand on the top edge of the bra cups to
hold them in place.

Be sure to have the cups right side out when
sewing them in. If the cups are too close together
for you, adjust by either adding elastic to the
end tabs or by inserting more elastic between
the cups.

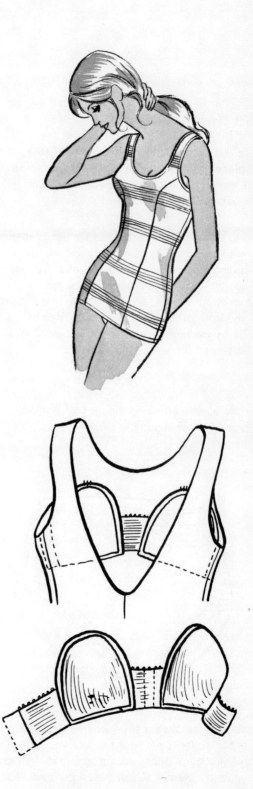

Ladies' Two-Piece Swimsuit

There are several small pattern pieces to a
two-piece swimsuit. It may be helpful for you to
mark the pieces with tape as you cut them
to avoid mixing them up.

Making a two-piece swimsuit is similar to making
a one-piece suit. The same technics are used
for cutting, sewing and lining. However, you must
cut two more pieces of elastic — one for the
bottom of the bra and one for the top of the shorts.
Get the correct lengths for these pieces of
elastic by measuring elastic around waist and
under bra so it feels comfortable.

Sew the elastic on using the technic outlined
for one-piece swimsuits.

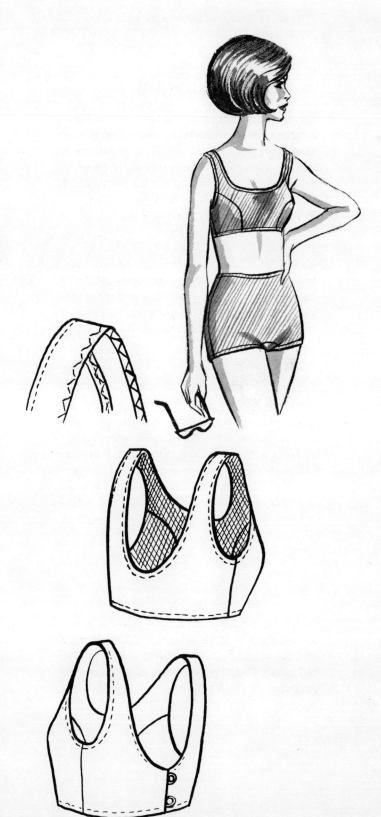

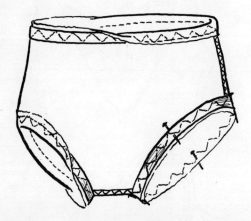

The bra or top of your two-piece swimsuit can
be either pulled over your head or you can cut
the center back open, adding about 1¼″ (3 cm.)
for seam allowance. Finish the center back with
hooks and eyes or buttons and button loops. If
you use buttons, you could add an individual touch
by using two small fancy buttons, for example.

Ladies' Bikini

SEW-KNIT-N-STRETCH has an easy-to-make
bikini swimsuit pattern. The bottom of the bikini
is made from just one pattern piece. However,
this pattern piece can be cut in two if your fabric
is not long enough. There is a dotted line on
the pattern piece at crotch. Be sure to add extra
fabric for seam allowance.

If the bra cups are too large for your bikini, trim
them to the size you require. After trimming, bind
the raw edges with seam binding. Fold the
binding double, insert raw edge of bra cup and
sew it on.

Use your imagination in adding your own
personal touch to your bikini. Some suggestions
are using spaghetti straps for shoulder straps,
inserting spaghetti straps (criss-cross fashion) at
side seams in shorts. Borrow ideas from the
ready-made bikinis — the extra little touches that
manufacturers add to the garment (as well as
the price tag).

Girls' One and Two-Piece Swimsuits

Use the same basic technics as outlined in swimsuits for ladies.

Making a little girl's swimsuit is even easier than making one for a lady. Remember that it is essential to have the greater stretch of the fabric go *around* the body. Be sure to line the entire swimsuit if your fabric is lightweight.

When making a girl's swimsuit for ages 8, 10 or 12, sew small bust darts to make the suit fit better (not necessary for smaller sizes).

It is not necessary to sew elastic around the arm openings and decolletage in a girl's swimsuit.* To get a perfect fit in the back, the back piece should be stretched from waist to arm opening as you are sewing the side seams.

After you have sewn the side seams, crotch and center back, try the swimsuit on the child and make any necessary adjustments to length by shortening or lengthening the shoulder straps using the same procedures as for ladies' one-piece swimsuits. Any changes or adjustments you make at this point should be indicated on your pattern pieces so the next swimsuit you make will be cut properly.

*If using swimsuit fabric that is too stretchy, sew elastic around arm openings and decolletage. This will prevent the swimsuit from gapping and being very uncomfortable.

Swimsuit Variations

You can have a lot of fun by creating your own individual swimsuits using the basic patterns. Here are a few suggestions you might want to try.

Contrasting Trim Instead of Elastic

Instead of using elastic around the arm openings and decolletage, use swimsuit fabric in a contrasting color, or the same color. If making a two-piece swimsuit, you might want to put the same color trim on the bottom of the bra, but here we suggest sliding a narrow elastic through the trim casing so the bra will stay in place.

Cut strips of swimsuit fabric approximately 1″ (2½ cm.) wide and slightly shorter than the lengths of elastic would be. Sew bands to form circles and try on. Fold the bands double lengthwise, wrong sides together. Place bands to openings, right sides and raw edges together. Sew to swimsuit using approximately ¼″ (6 mm.) seam allowance.

Accenting Lines on One-Piece Swimsuits

For an optical illusion on a one-piece swimsuit (to look slimmer), insert a contrasting color in the front side seams. Cut strips of fabric in a contrasting color as long as the front side seams, 1″ (2½ cm.) wide. Fold strips double lengthwise, wrong sides together, and insert them as you sew the front side seams. You may wish to use wider or narrower strips.

Swimsuit With Higher Back Decolletage

If you prefer a swimsuit that is not cut low in the back, cut your pattern piece as high as desired. However, be sure to make the elastic for the decolletage proportionately shorter.

A higher back decolletage usually requires a zipper in center back. You could also insert a zipper at center front. In this case, instead of placing center front on fold, add seam allowance and make a seam at center front, starting at bottom and ending where your zipper will be inserted.

Be sure the zipper you use is strong enough and also that it can be used in water. Remember to cut more seam allowance to allow for zipper insertion.

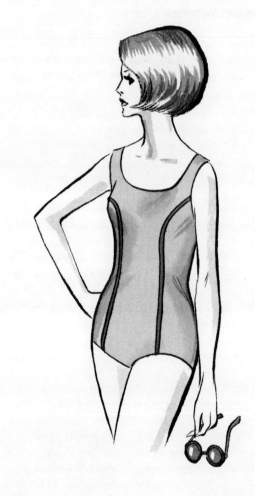

Belts for Swimsuits

On either one or two-piece swimsuits you can
add a belt for a special touch. Attach the belt about
1½″ (3½ cm.) from waistline or wherever you
desire. Cut a strip of fabric in the same color or
in a contrasting color approximately 2½″
(6½ cm.) wide and long enough to go around
the suit plus enough extra to work with. Sew
together and turn belt right side out. Make five
belt loops of swimsuit fabric approximately
⅜″ (1 cm.) wide when finished. Sew loops to
swimsuit: one, center back; two, side back;
two, side front. The belt can be fastened with
buttons and buttonholes, a buckle or it can be
tied. Be sure to use buttons and buckle that are
water-resistant.

Bra Variation for Two-Piece Swimsuit

If the center front of the bra is wider than you
like, here is an easy way to make it narrower.
Sew and turn a separate strip of fabric and
gather fabric between bra cups as tightly as you
wish. Fasten the strip by overlapping ends
and sewing them together. If you want to spend
a few more minutes, make permanent pleats or
gathers between the bra cups and secure them
by sewing one vertical seam. Now place the
separate strip over this seam and sew ends
together.

Appliques on Girls' Swimsuits

In adding a special touch to a little girl's swimsuit, you may want to attach an applique. Remember to make your applique out of swimsuit fabric. Draw the design you desire on a separate piece of swimsuit fabric in a contrasting color. Place this drawing on the swimsuit at point you wish it attached and sew a narrow zigzag seam around your design.

Cut off excess material as close as possible to stitches and sew around design again, over your first zigzag seam, using slightly wider zigzag stitch.

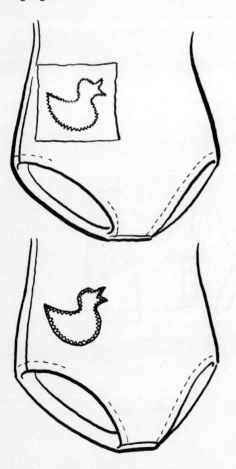

Personal Notes — Swimsuits

Sewing in a zipper can be done in several ways.
In this chapter we are going to describe two
methods that we think are the easiest. One is the
Overlap Zipper, and other is the Exposed Zipper
which is used when you don't have a seam.

Overlap Zipper

This method can be used wherever you have a
seam and would like to have a hidden zipper.

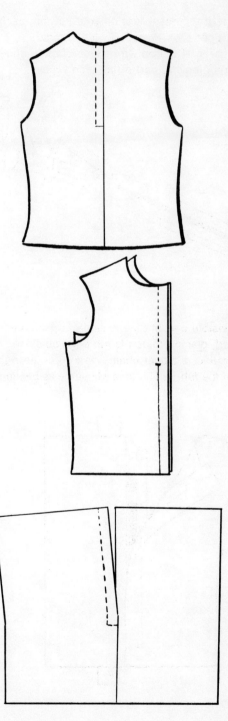

The first step after you have sewn the seam
to point where zipper will be inserted, is to baste
the zipper opening, enabling you to press
seam open evenly.

Now the basting has served its purpose, so you
can remove your stitches.

Sew a top stitch on the right side of fabric,
⅜″ (1 cm.) from side of opening.

Change the presser foot on your sewing machine to a zipper foot. Place "Scotch" Magic Transparent Tape on wrong side of cloth edge of zipper, leaving part of the tape visible.

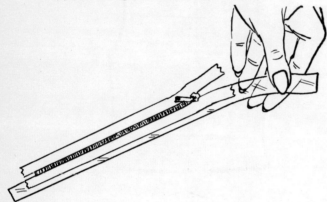

Turn up the seam allowance and sew in the fold (pressed crease) from wrong side. Sew from bottom to top of zipper.

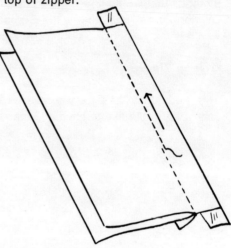

Stick visible part of tape to side of opening not stitched, placing folded fabric edge as close as possible to zipper chain. Work from the right side of the fabric. The tape will serve as basting.

Now you may remove the tape as it has served its purpose as basting.

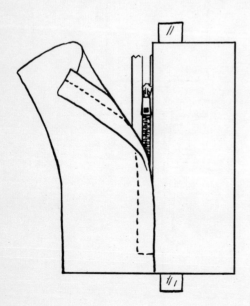

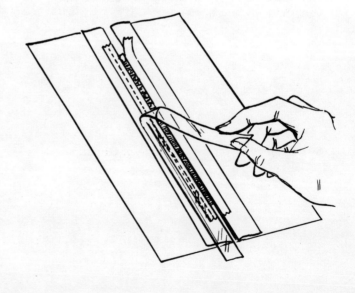

Place other side (stitched edge) of opening over zipper chain, hiding the zipper. Tape opening on right side of fabric, starting at the bottom.

Fold back fabric and sew as close as possible to stitching on seam allowance, starting at the bottom. If you open the zipper a little just before the seam is finished, the zipper slide will not be in your way.

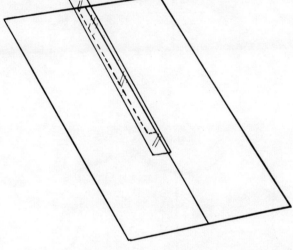

Remove the tape. Your zipper is inserted.

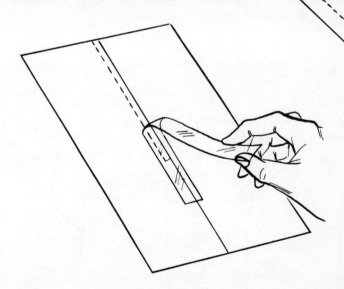

Exposed Zipper

This method is very good to use in a pullover
sweater where you have no seam to work with.
The zipper can be placed at center back or
front. This technic can be used with all types
of material.

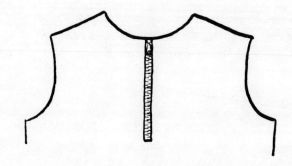

Mark center back or front where zipper is to be
inserted. Use "Scotch" Magic Transparent Tape
as a guide to cut zipper opening straight. Place
a piece of tape at the end of zipper opening to
avoid cutting the opening too long.

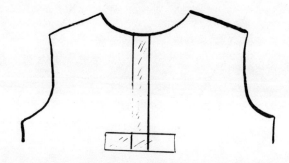

Cut opening and remove tape. If your fabric has
a tendency to ravel, overcast the edges.

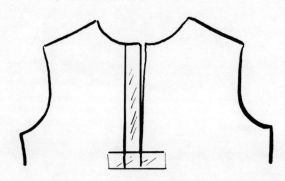

To keep fabric from stretching, place strips of tape about ½″ (1¼ cm.) from each side of opening.

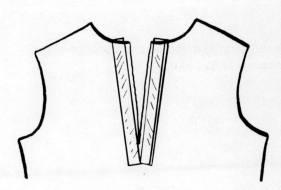

Place bottom of zipper at end of opening (right side of zipper to right side of fabric) so bottom of zipper chain is approximately ¼″ (6 mm.) from end of the opening. Baste end tabs of zipper with tape. Zipper is now lying in opposite direction from cut opening.

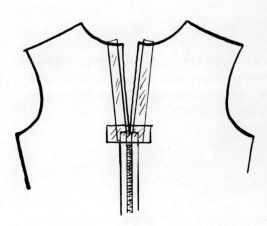

Fasten end of zipper to garment securely by sewing a few stitches the width of zipper chain.

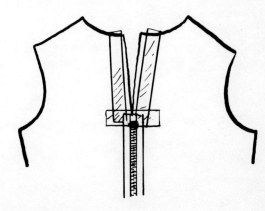

Remove tape on end tabs of zipper and turn zipper up into position.

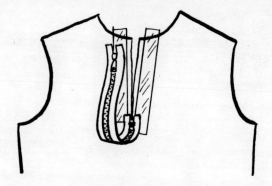

Fold one side of fabric over zipper and sew as close as possible to zipper chain (the seam allowance will be very narrow). Follow same procedure for other side.

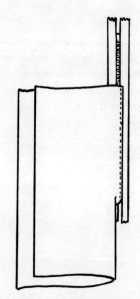

Now your zipper is inserted and you can put the neckband on your sweater. If desired, use hook and eye to finish.

Personal Notes — Zippers

In this chapter we will describe a few simple technics utilizing yarn in various ways to add special touches to the clothes you make. The decorations can be added before your seams are sewn or when the garment is finished, whichever you prefer.

These technics combined with your imagination can produce some really outstanding garments. We suggest using yarn made of the same material as the garment. For example, use orlon yarn on an orlon sweater, wool yarn on a wool sweater.

Yarn Border or Edge Decoration

This can be a very attractive addition using one or two lengths of yarn in colors that complement your garments. Arrange yarn on fabric and place under presser foot. Sew it to the garment with a wide zigzag stitch or a blindstitch. If you want a wider border, sew as many rows of yarn as you wish.

If you are using this type of decoration around the neck of a pullover, put a zipper in the back or front as the yarn will not stretch to go over your head.

Yarn Monogram

Children love to have their name or initials on
their clothes. You can do this very easily by
arranging the yarn on the fabric in the form of a
letter, and sewing a wide zigzag seam over
the yarn.

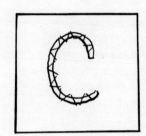

Yarn Flowers

You can make flowers out of yarn and decorate
garments in countless ways. Flowers can be sewn
around the neckline of a simple sweater, around
the hemline of a jacket, on the fronts of a
cardigan. The flowers can have leaves and stems
if you desire — they can be arranged singly or
in clusters or bouquets.

To make a flower, measure approximately 6″
(15 cm.) from end of yarn. Place yarn at this point
over top of a rod or pencil. Secure with "Scotch"
Magic Transparent Tape or a pin.

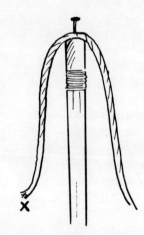

Holding end of yarn (X) to rod, wind yarn around
rod and yarn, starting about 1″ (2½ cm.) from
top. Each loop around the rod equals one petal
of your flower.

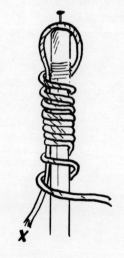

After you have enough loops around rod, remove it.

Put end X through top loop and pull end tight. This will form a circle of loops (the flower).

Tie securely and cut off ends.

Now your flower is ready to be attached to garment. This can be done by hand or if your sewing machine has an eyelet plate, place eyelet plate on top of the feed dog. Place fabric under sewing machine needle, poking the eyelet through fabric where you will place the middle of flower. Bring bobbin thread up through eyelet. The thread you are using will be the center of the flower, and can be the same color or a contrasting color. Set your sewing machine on wide zigzag stitch. Place center of flower directly over the eyelet. If you have a Viking (Husqvarna) sewing machine, use low gear at this point so you are able to control the speed. Sew a zigzag stitch as you slowly rotate the flower. If you have a button reed, use this now to hold petals flat while you sew the center.

Now your flower is completed and you are ready to make stem and leaves if you desire.

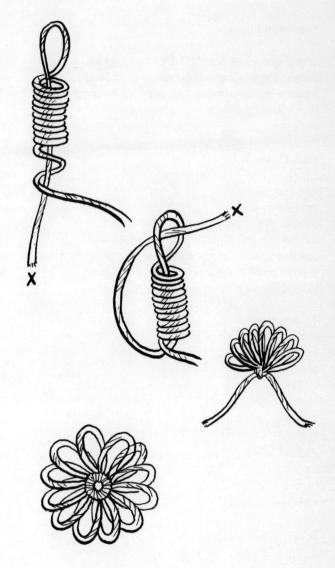

Stem and Leaves

Place yarn on fabric to form stem and leaves. Attach by sewing a blindstitch or wide zigzag stitch over the yarn, or sew them on by hand.

Pom-Pons

Children's clothes often call for special touches. Little balls made from yarn can be used in many ways on almost every article of clothing worn by children.

If you want the pom-pon to hang freely (as on a cap or bonnet), be sure to leave long ends of yarn after you have tied the knot.

Make a pom-pon by following the same procedure as for making a flower, only wind more yarn around the rod. Remember that the diameter of the rod equals the radius of the ball. Attach the pom-pon to garment in the same way you attach a flower. Now clip the loops, fluff up to form a pom-pon, and trim with scissors.

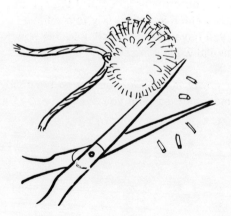

Yarn Fringe

Fringe is very easy to make and can add a
beautiful touch to jackets, sweaters, etc. It can
be made as wide and as long as you wish.
You can use only one color in your fringe or as
many colors as you desire. The fringe can either
be sewn in a seam or the entire width can be
exposed. The easiest way to make fringe is
with a weaver's reed.

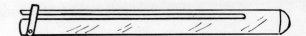

If you want your fringe wider than the weaver's
reed, you can tape a piece of cardboard to
the edge increasing the width of the fringe as
much as you want.

First, tape end of yarn to top of weaver's reed (this will enable you to keep track of the end and will make it a little easier to handle). Now starting at the top, wind yarn around weaver's reed. The thickness of your fringe will depend on how close you wind the yarn. Place weaver's reed over fabric where you want your fringe and sew seam on your sewing machine in weaver's reed slit.

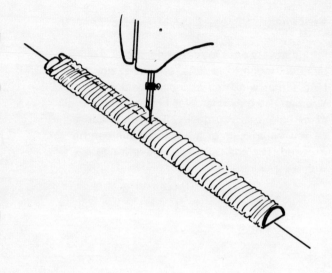

You can make your length of fringe as long as you want by unlocking the top of weaver's reed, sliding sewn fringe over top, pulling reed toward you (but still leaving it under the presser foot), and continue winding and sewing.

When you have sewn the length of fringe you require, remove the weaver's reed. You can either leave the fringe in loops, or cut them open.

Fringe Sewn in Seam

On a jacket, for example, fringe sewn in the front seam and around the neckline can be very chic. To do this, follow the preceding steps for winding the yarn, but place the weaver's reed on right side of fabric using ¼″ (6 mm.) seam allowance, long loops facing the side seam. Sew the fringe and remove the weaver's reed. Now place facing over fringe, right sides together. The fringe is now between fabric and facing. Sew a seam using ¼″ (6 mm.) seam allowance through all three thicknesses (fabric, fringe and facing).

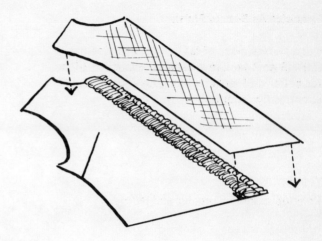

Turn facing to wrong side and press. The fringe is now the finished edge of your seam. You can cut the loops or leave them — whichever you wish.

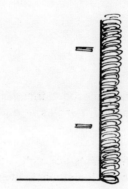

Extra Touch Where Entire Fringe Is Exposed

You can use the fringe as a bottom finish. Place the weaver's reed and yarn on desired hemline and sew fringe on right side of fabric. Hem and press.

Exposed fringe can be even more attractive by sewing one or two pieces of yarn over the seam on fringe by using a zigzag stitch. This yarn can be the same color as your fringe or contrasting colors.

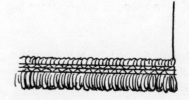

Triangles As Bottom Finish

Cut a square piece of fabric. (As a suggestion, a 2″ (5 cm.) square makes an attractive triangle for bottoms of jackets). Fold the square double, wrong sides together.

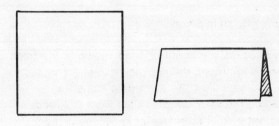

Fold top corners to center and tape.

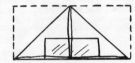

Make as many triangles as you need to trim the garment. You can overlap the triangles or place them end to end.

Baste triangles to hemline (points up), right sides together, and sew them on with a straight stitch.

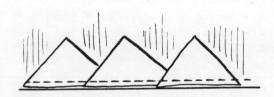

Remove tape. Turn triangles down, press and hem.

These triangles used as a bottom edge add a beautiful touch to shells and jackets. You can use your imagination for interesting color combinations and they are very smart when made from the same color as the garment.

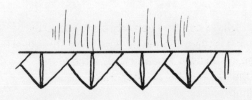

Personal Notes — Yarn Work and Decorations

_____

_____

_____

_____

_____

_____

_____

_____

_____

_____

_____

_____

_____

_____

_____

_____

Here are some ideas I hope will be useful to you.
Some are my own, some I've picked up in my
travels throughout Europe and the United States.
These shortcuts have been invaluable to me
in my work and in sewing my own clothes.
They apply not only to working with knit and
stretch fabric, but also to many other types
of material.

How to Get a Straight Hemline

Pull a length of string along a piece of white
chalk, coating it with chalk dust. Stretch this
chalk-coated string between doorjams at exact
height you want your hemline. ("Scotch" Magic
Transparent Tape will hold string to doorjams
and leave no marks on your woodwork). Stand
next to this chalk-coated string with your
garment on and turn around slowly. You will have
a 100% straight chalkline to use as your hemline
guide. Chalk can be easily brushed off fabric.
If you prefer you can place the string where you
are going to cut the hem.

If you measure the distance from floor to string,
you will always be able to obtain your correct
hemline.

How to Get a Straight Line

I think that everyone will agree that sewing,
cutting or folding a 100% straight line presents
quite a problem. Very few people are able to
cut a straight line with no guide other than their
eyes, let alone sew a straight seam. So here
are some easy technics I have been using.
They are fast and accurate and I think you will
also find them very helpful.

For example, when you are sewing a side seam
or making pleats, take a coarse thread (such
as crochet thread) and coat it with chalk. Tie one
end of the thread around a pin and stake the
pin at an angle at the point you wish your
straight line to begin. Hold the other end of the
thread taut directly on point you want your
straight line to end. Now, lift this taut thread
straight up about ½″ (1¼ cm.) and let it snap
back on the fabric.

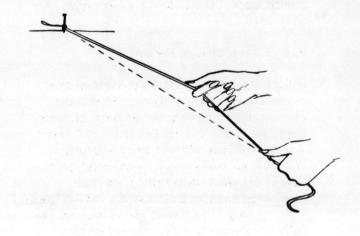

You will have a straight line of chalk dust to use
as a guide. (The chalk dust can easily be
brushed off the fabric).

To get a straight line on non-stretch fabric such
as cotton, silk, etc., simply place an ordinary pin
on point where you want your line to begin.
Then, holding the pin rigid with one hand fabric
taut with the other hand, draw pin rapidly across
fabric. The pin will naturally follow a fabric
thread.

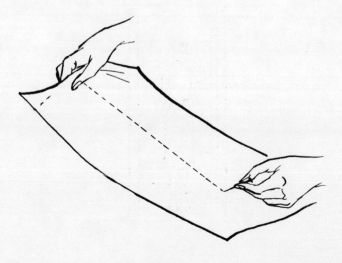

Now you have a guide for a straight line that
you can fold for a pleat or use for a sewing or
cutting guide.

How to Sew Perfect Darts

It's easy to understand why making darts can be difficult. Darts are always sewn on the bias and therefore you have no fabric thread to follow as a guide. Here's another place you can use "Scotch" Magic Transparent Tape.

Place a piece of tape on edge of dart line and sew the dart using the tape edge as a guide. Remove the tape. It leaves no marks on the fabric unless fabric has a high nap (such as velvet or velour).

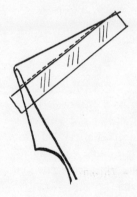

Sometimes the garments we sew call for exposed darts — for example on the front of a blouse for a decoration. Or maybe you are sewing darts on some type of lightweight sheer fabric and experience has shown you that locking the dart thread will cause the fabric to pull and pucker.

It's possible and very simple to make a dart without having to lock the threads at all at the dart point.

To do this, thread your sewing machine backwards. That is, take the bobbin thread through the needle on your sewing machine and proceed on up the machine to the spool. You now have only one thread — there are no two threads to lock. You may find it easier to thread the machine backwards by tying the bobbin thread and top thread together (with a very small knot). Pull this knot through the sewing machine needle and on up the machine to the spool. Be sure to leave enough thread wound around spool for your dart.

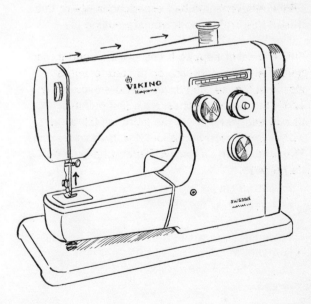

Start sewing at dart point.

How to Gather With Round Elastic

Place elastic under presser foot. Sew a zigzag
seam wide enough to go over elastic (but don't
sew on the elastic itself). Now pull end of
elastic to get as much fullness as you require.

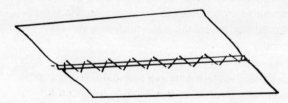

How to Gather With a Thread

The usual way of gathering fabric is to sew with
long stitches and pull a thread to obtain gathers.
I think everyone has had experiences where this
thread has broken while you are pulling it.

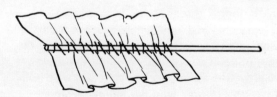

This will never happen if you sew a strong thread
(such as crochet thread) on the fabric with a
zigzag stitch, so the strong thread moves freely
under the zigzag stitches. Now, just pull this
thread and you can get the fabric as full as you
want without worrying about the thread breaking.
This thread can be removed after it has served
its purpose.

How to Avoid Baggy Knees on Slacks

Nearly everyone at some time or other has had
experience with baggy knees in slacks or
trousers. Slacks with baggy knees can certainly
spoil an otherwise attractive outfit but they will
be a thing of the past by doing this.

From non-stretch, lightweight fabric, cut out
knee-size pieces. Attach these pieces to wrong
side of slacks at inside and outside seams,
over the knees.

I have seen this type of knee lining in very
expensive slacks from some of the fashion houses
in Europe, and I can say from my personal
experience that it works beautifully. (Just be sure
you don't get your foot caught in the lining).

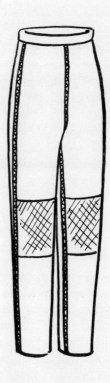

How to Renew Thread

If the thread you presently have in your home
tends to break easily, this could be due to low
humidity. This thread may be renewed by placing
it near steam (such as in the bathroom when
you are taking a bath).

How to Sew on Plastic

Plastic has always been a problem to sew
because the needle usually makes big holes and
the seams ripple.

Eliminate this easily and efficiently by placing
a little sewing machine oil on your finger, sliding
finger in front of needle as you sew. You'll be
pleasantly surprised to see what a little
oil can do.

It will also help to use a roller presser foot which
works on vinyl as well.

How to Match Checks, Plaids, Stripes

Many women will not even attempt to sew
garments of these attractive patterns because
they are afraid they will not be able to line up the
seams properly. This is unfortunate but very
understandable. Sewing with plaids, stripes, etc.
can be very discouraging because you can cut
the fabric so it matches perfectly, but after you
sew the seam you find something went wrong.
What usually happens is that the fabric slides
a little and even a slight misalignment is enough
to ruin your seam.

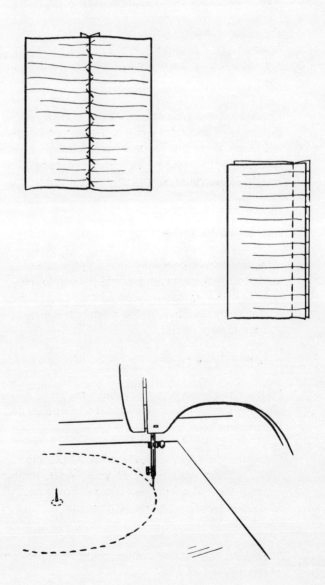

Here's how to get a perfectly matched seam.
First fold and press seam allowances to wrong
side. Then turn fabric over to right side and
perfect seam by lining up your pattern. Now baste
the pieces together on the right side using a
very narrow zigzag stitch — as long as possible —
with loose tension (so you can easily pull out
the stitches). With this zigzag basting stitch you
will pick up perhaps only one thread on each
side, and all the while you will be able to control
the pattern matching. Now you turn it over to
wrong side, open seam allowances and sew your
seam on the fold using normal stitch length.
All that remains is to remove the zigzag basting
stitches. I think you will be very pleased at
how well this works.

How to Sew a Circle

Secure a thumb tack flat to your sewing machine
or cabinet (point sticking up) with "Scotch" Magic
Transparent Tape. The distance from tack to
sewing machine needle will be the radius of your
circle. Poke the tack through fabric and pivot
fabric around the tack, sewing as you go.
You will have an accurate circle.

How to Make Belt Loops and Button Loops

Making belt loops and button loops is time-consuming when you either crochet them or sew a loop from the fabric (and it's always hard to get fabric loops as narrow as you would like). Here is a simple way to get a more professional-looking loop and it will take a fraction of the time.

Take heavy crochet thread and sew a zigzag seam over the thread, pulling the thread back and forth under the presser foot a few times till the thread is completely covered with stitches. Your setting has to be for narrow and close zigzag.

An easy way to attach belt loops to a garment (if you don't sew them in the seam) is to cut the length you need for each belt loop, plus enough extra to work with. Then with a rather large needle, poke ends of loop through to wrong side of fabric and make knots to hold ends securely.

The following technic works very well for attaching button loops:

Place the loops between facing and fabric when sewing front seam. Turn, press, and you will have a very professional-looking job.

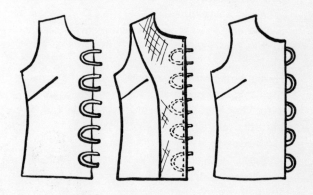

How to Change Waistband Elastic

Here is the fastest and easiest way to replace elastic in waistbands. Cut new elastic to correct length. Then, at small opening in waistband casing, pull out loop of old elastic and snip it. Now fasten end of new elastic to end of old elastic with safety pin. Pull old elastic out — new elastic in! Sew ends of new elastic together and your elastic is replaced.

Personal Notes

Personal Notes

Personal Notes

_____

_____

_____

_____

_____

_____

_____

_____

_____

_____

_____

_____

_____

_____

_____

_____

Personal Notes